PETER DAWKINS

Shakespeare's Wisdom

in

As You Like It

I. C. Media Productions

Published by I C Media Productions
Warwickshire United Kingdom

ISBN 0–9532890–1–X

Typeset by Starnine Design
Printed in England by Biddles Ltd, Guildford.

Contents

Dedication

This book I dedicate to my friends.

Acknowledgements

I would like to thank all my friends who have helped make this book possible, and in particular the following people: the 'Roses' team who have assisted me, edited, illustrated, and helped design and prepare the book for publishing—my wife Sarah, my son Samuel, Michèle Beaufoy, Geralyn Walsh, Scott Oldham and Suzy Straw; my 'professional' friends who have given me encouragement, information and ideas—Mark Rylance (actor and Artistic Director of the Shakespeare Globe Theatre), Claire van Kampen (Director of Music and Artistic Assistant of the Shakespeare Globe Theatre), Hugh Young (actor-director of Daylight Theatre) and Jill Line MA (Lecturer in Shakespeare); and my 'supportive' friends who have helped make this venture financially possible—Gay Browning, Francis McKeagney, Mary Walsh, Diana Myers, Mary Pout and Diana Tinson.

Illustrations

Diagrams by Samuel Dawkins.
Cover illustration and chapter headpieces by Michèle Beaufoy.
Cover designed by Gerald Beckwith, Starnine Design.
Photograph on back cover by Dominic McManus.

Textual Note

All quotations from Shakespeare's *As You Like It* are based on the Arden Shakespeare (1955/9), edited by John Russell Brown, but with some capitals and original spelling from the 1st Folio reinstated where appropriate.All quotations from the Bible are taken from The Companion Bible (1974), being the Authorised Version of 1611 as published by the Revisers in their 'Parallel Bible' in 1885.

Introduction

The 'Wisdom of Shakespeare' Series

This series on the Wisdom of Shakespeare is designed to investigate and make known some of the extraordinary wisdom, knowledge and philosophy contained in the Shakespeare plays.

Besides the plays themselves, a clue to the greatness of Shakespeare in this respect is given by Ben Jonson in his tribute to the Author prefacing the Shakespeare 1st Folio of 1623, as also by the inscription on the contemporaneous Shakespeare Monument.

On the Shakespeare Monument, erected *c.* 1620-23 in Holy Trinity Church at Stratford-upon-Avon, Warwickshire, to honour the memory of Shakespeare, the great Bard is referred to (in Latin) as 'A Pylus in judgment, a Socrates in genius, a Maro in art'.

Pylus was the appellation of Nestor, King of Pylus, one of the Argonauts who went in search of the golden fleece and who was the most perfect of Homer's heroes in the Trojan war. As a statesman, ruler and judge, Pylus was renowned for his eloquence, address, wisdom, justice and prudence of mind.

Socrates was the most celebrated philosopher of Greece and a renowned orator. The Delphic Oracle proclaimed him as the wisest of mankind. He was the principal instigator of the great philosophies that have constituted the major traditions of Western civilisation since his time, and was the advocate of clarity and the inductive procedure, for which he was particularly famed. His great aim was the happiness and good of his countrymen, and the reformation of their corrupted morals. By introducing moral philosophy he induced people to consider themselves, their passions, their opinions, their duties, faculties and actions. He used drama to aid him in this, and the theatrical tragedies of his pupil Euripides are said to have been at least partly composed by him, although he remained hidden as a playwright behind the mask of his pupil.

Maro was the surname of Virgil, the greatest of the Roman poets. He was known as the prince of poets and Homer's successor. He was not only a highly learned scholar and refined writer, but also a high initiate of the Orphic Mysteries as practised at Naples, where he lived for the last part of his life. His *Æneid* was based upon the Mysteries and Homer's epic tales, the *Iliad* and *Odyssey*.

For Shakespeare to be likened to these three illustrious men—not just one, but all three—is an enormous complement, and the inferences say a great deal about the Bard.

This viewpoint is supported by Ben Jonson, a renowned playwright and poet in his own right. In his tributory poem to Shakespeare prefacing the Shakespeare 1st Folio, Jonson refers to his 'beloved' friend as an Apollo and Mercury, and as the 'Sweet Swan of Avon'. Furthermore, implying that Shakespeare was, like him, a noted classical scholar, he declares in his tribute that even if Shakespeare had small Latin and less Greek, he (Ben) would still honour him, calling forth the great Roman and Greek tragedians to hear and applaud his tragedies. As for comedies, Ben can think of no one of the ancient Greeks or Romans who even approaches Shakespeare: he is alone, supreme.

To be likened to the gods Apollo and Mercury, rather than just inspired by them, is a mighty tribute, particularly as coming from the talented and critical poet laureate, Ben Jonson. Apollo is the god of poetic inspiration and illumination, and leader of the choir of Muses. Mercury is the god of eloquence and learning.

The 'sweet swan' is a reference to the singing swan, which is sweetest when singing its own 'swan-song'. This was the symbol of Orpheus, musician to the Argonauts and the originator of the Orphic Mysteries that subsequently became the wisdom teachings and Mysteries of Classical Greece and Rome. These Mysteries formed the foundations of Classical philosophy and of all Platonic and Neoplatonic thought. Orpheus was considered to be the representative of Bacchus, the god of Drama, whose drama was in particular the Mysteries that were performed by the bacchants, bacchantes and *eumolpoi* ('good singers'), the initiates and hierophants of the Orphic Mysteries. Both comedy and drama, and theatre as such, derive from the Bacchanalian Mysteries. Moreover, the white swan, symbol of Orpheus and the *Eumolpoi,* is an emblem of Apollo.

Mercury (Roman *Mercurius*) is derived from the Ancient Egyptian *Maa Kheru,* meaning 'the True Word' and 'he who is of true voice'. It was a title bestowed on the high initiates of the Egyptian Mysteries—*i.e.* those who had sung their 'swan-song' and undergone psychological death and rebirth. The title continued to be used in the Classical Mysteries. Another Greek name for Mercury was Hermes Trismegistus (*i.e.* Hermes the Thrice Greatest), but this title was applied specifically to the greatest of all the initiates in any epoch. From this name comes the term 'Hermetic' for the great wisdom teachings and developing philosophical thought that have been handed on from the time of the Ancient Egyptians to successive generations and cultures, and of which we are inheritors today via the Neoplatonism of the Renaissance and the great poetry of Shakespeare.

The works of Shakespeare declare him to be one of the greatest, if not *the* greatest, of the Neoplatonists. His plays are suffused with Renaissance Neoplatonism. To understand this is to understand Shakespeare.

Renaissance Neoplatonism

The founders of Renaissance Neoplatonism were Marsilio Ficino and Giovanni Pico della Mirandola, both members of the brilliant circle of scholars, writers and artists associated with the Medici court in Florence in the 15th century, under the patronage of the great Cosimo de' Medici.

Marsilio Ficino (1433-99), a scholar, physician and priest, was commissioned by Cosimo to translate into Latin the Hermetic writings and the dialogues of Plato, together with the Neoplatonic writings of Porphyry, Proclus, Pseudo-Dionysus the Areopagite and Plotinus. The translation of the *Corpus Hermeticum* was ready in 1464 and published in 1471 under the title of *Pimander*, and the translations of Plato's dialogues, completed *c.* 1468, were published as the *Platonic Theology* in 1474.

Ficino's understanding, as that of others including St. Augustine, was that a divine theology or wisdom tradition, based on love, began simultaneously with Zoroaster among the Persians and with Hermes Trismegistus (*i.e.* Thoth) among the Egyptians. They believed that this wisdom tradition led in an unbroken chain to Plato via Orpheus and Pythagorus. It is this wisdom which is reputed to underlie the Hebrew, Orphic and Christian teachings, all of which developed from the blended Hermetic and Magian origin.

Demonstrating that this wisdom tradition was associated with Christianity, with links via Moses and the

Zoroastrian Magi, Ficino was able to reconcile Platonic and neo-Platonic philosophy with Christian theology. He regarded both philosophy and religion as being manifestations of a spiritual life, each needing the other in order to attain the *summum bonum* or greatest good.

According to the Neoplatonic philosophy which Ficino founded, love is the sustaining principle of the universe, and the attainment of the highest good is dependant not upon the Church but upon an impulse universal to man. The soul is not only immortal, but all souls by an inner urge naturally seek truth and goodness.

Ficino was immeasurably helped in the development of Neoplatonism by Giovanni Pico della Mirandola (1463-94). Pico joined Ficino's circle in 1484 and introduced Cabala into Ficino's Neoplatonism, being the founder or first great exponent of Christian Cabala. In this Pico was following in the footsteps of the poet-philosopher Ramon Lull, who in the 13th century, in Spain, brought together Jewish Cabala, Islamic mysticism and Christian revelation into a single method, which had an enormous influence on succeeding generations. As a result of Pico's and Ficino's partnership, Neoplatonism became a universal philosophy, which blended Hebrew Cabala with the Hermetic, Neoplatonic and Christian teachings, making a synthesis of them all. As a result, the spiritual, magical and scientific core of Renaissance Neoplatonism was born.

Having travelled from Italy into France, this Renaissance Neoplatonism took a strong hold in England in the 16th century, beginning in King Henry VIII's time and reaching a zenith during the reign of Queen Elizabeth I, particularly in the works of William Shakespeare.

The Bible

Shakespeare's knowledge of the Bible is remarkably extensive and detailed. The teachings of the Bible underlie all his plays to such a degree that the plays seem, in fact, to be dramatised commentaries on the Bible teachings, aided by Cabalistic philosophy and Hermetic wisdom as well as by Shakespeare's extraordinary observation, insight into and knowledge of human nature.

Not for nothing then, it would seem, was an Englishman urged to possess a copy of both the Bible and the Shakespeare plays, and to always carry them with him when travelling.

The Teacher

Not only is Shakespeare a great poet, dramatist, Neoplatonic philosopher and Christian cabalist, but he is also a supreme teacher who teaches through entertainment, following the path of the ancients:

> The wisdom of the ancients devised a way of inducing men to study truth by means of pious frauds, the delicate Minerva secretly lurking beneath the mask of pleasure.[1]

Minerva is the Roman name for the Greek goddess of wisdom, Pallas Athena, the Tenth (and Chief) Muse, and the especial muse of Shakespeare. Her Greek name literally means 'Spear Shaker', and she was renowned for shaking her spear of light at dark ignorance, exactly as Ben Jonson says of Shakespeare in his Folio tribute:

> For a good Poet's made, as well as borne.
> And such wert thou. Looke how the father's face

Lives in his issue, even so, the race
Of Shakespeare's minde, and manners brightly shines
In his well torned, and true filed lines:
In each of which, he seemes to shake a Lance,
As brandish't at the eyes of Ignorance.

The intention and hope of this series is to help reveal to lovers of Shakespeare some of the extraordinary and brilliant light concealed in Shakespeare's plays, and to pay homage to one who has been an exceptional friend and teacher to me and countless others—the great English Bard.

Foreword by Mark Rylance

I would guess that Wisdom is the marriage of love with knowledge. For wisdom, as I have experienced it, is knowledge shared in the right way at the right time to be of benefit; and love, intuitive love, may be the only guide as to how and when one speaks with benefit.

Shakespeare didn't bother too much with the printed page it seems, trusting his knowledge to the voices and ears of the theatre, which only survives by an intuitive sense of timing with present circumstance. This 400 years of readjustment of the form which Shakespeare's knowledge takes has kept alive his ability to be wise. It is difficult to imagine Rosalind curing Orlando of his love sickness, or Jaques cleansing *'the foul body of th' infected world'* merely by means of a book. Both characters invest themselves in the motley of disguise, one as Ganymede, one as a fool, because play-acting such as this gives one the ability to be speaking and also listening at the same time. The sense of timing and awareness great Lovers and Fools develop from this listening enables them to speak with devastating benefit.

Peter Dawkins too has shared his knowledge orally up to this point, speaking with a listening ear directly to small groups, judging moment by moment when and how to speak. I have listened and spoken about Shakespeare with Peter Dawkins for the past ten years. He has advised on no less than ten separate productions in Britain and America, including this year's *As You Like It* in the Globe. Although his ideas are mercurial, constantly changing shape as our times change and the plays themselves reflect different meanings, they continue to spring faithfully from a Jovial wisdom about Love, which I have found to be at the heart and core of Shakespeare.

I am delighted that he is publishing his ideas on Shakespeare's plays for the first time in this Wisdom of Shakespeare Series, as they have more than any other single factor - apart from playing in the Globe - increased my understanding and enjoyment of Shakespeare, but I am also aware that this book cannot listen to you, it cannot apply its author's timing, or care to match his knowledge to the degree of desire with which you wish to question.

Peter's way is to explore the underlying structure of the plays which imitate the underlying structure of life itself as interpreted by such traditions as that of the Kabala, Hermeticism or Alchemy, and other teachings from the Western Mystery Tradition. In these traditions, it was important not only for the mind to be inspired by what it saw and heard, but also for the emotions to be stirred and moved. Read imaginatively, this book can be a path for lovers out of the court and up to the discernable edge of the deepest forests of Shakespeare. But you must still then enter the unknown dark and listen in your heart for your own motleyed Shakespeare, page and hidden princess, until you cry out in despair with Orlando, *'I can no longer live by thinking'!*

Whether you are an actor person like me reading this book to help you play on the stage, or an actual person reading to help you play in the yards and galleries of the Globe, *As You Like It* lives as you are like it—and as you are like it will it be as you like it.

M. R.

Author's Preface

The purpose of this book is to provide an insight into the surprising depth of wisdom and philosophy which is waiting to be discovered behind the romantic façade of *As You Like It*.

As You Like It is one of the most popular light-hearted and fun Shakespeare plays, set in a highly romanticised Arcadian dream-world. It is pure fairy-tale—or so it seems on the surface. Not far beneath the surface is a historical reality of sorts, including political, social and psychological matters which still concern us now, when our imagination can suitably translate them into modern terms. For the most part, however, the play is treated by audiences as a romantic and highly entertaining fairy-tale, having a magic which somehow continues to make the play pertinent and enjoyable today. What that magic might be is what this book investigates.

Deeper beneath the surface of the play can be found truths about the human soul and the journey (or journeys) we each take through life. Keys given in the story-line, in the speeches of the play, open the doors to the world of the magician. Rosalind even talks about being conversant with a great magician who lies hidden in the forest. Who or what is this magician that lies therein, and what is the magic?

For the plan of the book, I begin with a sketch of the play's background history, to set the scene in terms of the writing of the play. This is followed by a chapter summarising the story of the play, scene by scene. This is for the benefit of those who do not know the play or do not know it very well, but it could be helpful also to a reader who is conversant with the play, as it deliberately picks out the key points which will be discussed in the book.

After laying out the background and story in the first two chapters, the rest of the book delves into the deeper matter of the play, step by step. First there is a chapter identifying the major plots and themes. This is then followed by a chapter on some initiatory themes in the story which relate to those allegorised in certain myths and fairytales. The fifth chapter outlines the sequential cycles of initiation hidden in the story, which create its real structure and purpose. Together with this is an explanation of what initiation means in the context of the play. The following two chapters continue by providing a more detailed description and explanation of each cycle, and an in-depth discussion of the key philosophical points.

Finally, to conclude the book are three chapters indicating the special significance of Shakespeare's choice and use of location, the importance and meaning of the names of the characters, and how the Hebraic and Christian Cabala underlies the play. The final chapter on the Cabala focuses on what is called the 'Tree of Life', with an explanation of what it means and how it can be used to understand the play, to understand life generally and to understand ourselves.

I have used the Arden edition of *As You Like It* when quoting from the play, which I highly recommend both for its text and its notes. I have also used the Companion Bible for biblical references, which are many, since the play is almost a text-book on the Bible. I recommend that the earnest reader has a copy of these two source books (or their equivalents) at hand when they read this book, in order to get the most from what I have written.

I have not attempted to provide a bibliography, except for the references which annotate the book. Some people may call this remiss; but there are many excellent books available in bookshops and libraries, both modern and ancient, all of which I certainly have not read although I have read and studied extensively! My suggestion is to follow your own intuitions and inspirations in this matter, based on the knowledge you already have. The matter we are dealing with is Renaissance Neoplatonism, itself derived primarily from Christian, Hebraic, Neoplatonic and Platonic, Pythagorean, Orphic, Hermetic, Ancient Egyptian, Magian and Druidic sources.

Finally, I wish you joy in your reading and hope that you will find this book useful. To search for truth seems to be one of the pleasures of life, for nearly all of us have an in-built natural curiosity to know. When what we discover is actually illuminating and useful in our lives, then it really is a joy. It is this joy that I wish for you, and the pleasure of enjoying Shakespeare's works of art even more than before.

P. D.

1. Background

*A*s *You Like It* was probably written sometime between 1598 and 1600. It does not appear in Francis Mere's list of Shakespeare plays, which he gives in his *Palladis Tamia, Wits Treasury*, published in 1598, but it was entered in the Stationer's Register on 4th August 1600. The play was registered together with two other Shakespeare plays, *Henry V* and *Much Ado About Nothing*, and Ben Jonson's comedy, *Every Man in his Humour*. These were entered as books 'to be staied', implying that there was a threat of piracy and the Lord Chamberlain's Company acted to assert their copyright. However, *As You Like It* never appeared in quarto. Its first appearance in print was in the Shakespeare 1st Folio of 1623.

There is a theory suggesting that *As You Like It* was written by Shakespeare initially for private performance at the marriage of Henry Wriothesley, the Earl of Southampton, to Elizabeth Vernon, one of the Queen's ladies-in-waiting, in 1598.[1] This theory supposes that this is the reason for the inclusion of the wedding masque in the play and why Meres does not mention *As You Like It* in his list, as, being privately performed, he may not have known of its existence. This theory, however, is unsubstantiated.

About this time, 1598-1600, there was a temporary revival of interest in the Arcadian pastoral and woodland theme, with its idea of a golden or naturalistic and care-free age—one filled with love and adventure. This included renewed enthusiasm for the euphuistic plays of John Lyly. There was also a parallel interest in the associated mythology of Robin Hood and his merry men, living in the Forest of Sherwood. In 1598, for instance, there were two plays about Robin Hood in performance at the Rose theatre, by the Lord Admiral's Men, which were very popular—*The Downfall of Robert Earl of Huntingdon* by Anthony Munday, and *The Death of Robert Earl of Huntingdon* by Munday and Chettle. *As You Like It* would seem to have been written in the wave of this enthusiasm.

Shakespeare's play has an Arcadian setting in the Forest of Arden, and includes references to Robin Hood. The Forest of Arden in the play is actually the anglicised form of the Forest of Ardennes, a hilly, wooded but pastoral region on the borders of France, Belgium and Luxembourg. It was referred to in poetry on pastoral and Arcadian themes, and was especially made famous in this context because of its use as a romantic setting in Ludovic Ariosto's popular book, *Orlando Furioso*. By using the Ardennes, Shakespeare was following his main story source, Thomas Lodge's *Rosalynde*, and, to suit this, he makes reference to characters in the play as being French, such as Orlando, who is called 'the stubbornest young fellow of France', and Amiens and Le Beau who have French names. Moreover, the hunting, love-making, formalities and sparkling repartee of the play is an accurate and perceptive representation of the culture of 16th century France, ruled over by the Valois court and French nobility. In this respect the play closely parallels Shakespeare's earlier comedy, *Love's Labour's Lost*, which is likewise set in France amongst the French aristocracy. However, Shakespeare's Forest of Arden is also connected with the English Forest of Arden and the famous outlaw, Robin Hood, both historically and symbolically.

The English Forest of Arden no longer existed as a forest in Shakespeare's time, but many centuries earlier it had covered most of what later became Warwickshire, from the river Avon valley northwards to the site of Birmingham. South of the Avon the ancient forest joined another forest covering a large part of the Cotswolds, which became known as the Whychwoods, home of the Huicca tribe and the *huiccas* or witches (*i.e.* wise people) of old. Robin Hood was originally Robin of Loxley, his parent's home being at Loxley, situated a few miles south of Warwick in what was once the Forest of Arden and close to the ancient Huicca territory.

In addition to the Robin Hood and Arcadian themes, the inclusion in the play by Shakespeare of the satirical Jaques, which allows a discussion on the ethics of satire, was also of contemporary topical interest. Satirical writing was the source of much heated argument during 1598-9, and in June 1599 an act for the suppression of satirical writing was passed, leading to the burning of Nashe's and Harvey's vitriolic pamphlets.

The Globe theatre opened in Spring 1599, and it is possible that *As You Like It* was written especially for the newly erected playhouse, with Jaques telling the audience that 'all the world's a stage'. Like Shakespeare's contemporaneous *Henry V*, with its opening reference to the 'wooden O', it would have been most appropriate.

In a Jacobean revival, *As You Like It* is thought to have been played before King James I at Wilton, seat of the Pembrokes, in 1603. A letter of 1603, from Mary (*née* Sidney), Lady Pembroke, to her son, William Herbert, the 3rd Earl, asking him to bring the King from Salisbury to see a performance of *As You Like It* at Wilton House, is unfortunately missing.[3] The letter is reputed to have mentioned that, 'We have the man Shakespeare with us'. The court was indeed at Salisbury at that time, to avoid the plague in London, and a possible corroboration of the story is given by the Chamber Accounts of December 1603, which record a payment to John Heminge, on behalf of the Lord Chamberlain's Company, for coming to Wilton 'and there presenting before His Maiestie an playe'.[4]

The major source for *As You Like It* appears to have been Thomas Lodge's prose romance, *Rosalynde*, a new edition of which was published in 1598. It had been published first in 1590, and then again in 1592 and 1596. The intriguing title-page of this work reads:

> Rosalynde. Eupheus golden legacie: found after his death in his Cell at Silexedra. Bequeathed to Philautus sonnes noursed up with their father in England. Fetcht from the Canaries. By T. L. Gent.

The author declares, in the Dedication to the Lord Chamberlain, Lord Hunsdon, to have written the novel 'to beguile the time' whilst on a voyage 'to the islands of Terceras and the Canaries' with Captain Clarke, in 1586-7. He mentions the work as being 'hatched in the storms of the ocean, and feathered in the surges of many perilous seas'.

Euphues is from the Greek, meaning 'well-grown', and was a name used by John Lyly for his literary hero and adopted by a group of writers who studied at Oxford in the 1570's, under the tutelage of John Rainoldes. The name was applied, as Euphuism, to a style of writing that they developed—an epigrammatic, witty and elaborately balanced style which they had first learned at Oxford.[5] Lodge was one of the original euphuists, but the novelist and playwright, John Lyly (1554-1606), became the most

Rosalynde.

Euphues golden le-

gacie: found after his death
in his Cell at Si-
lexedra.

Bequeathed to Philautus sonnes
nourſed vp with their
father in Eng-
land.

Fetcht from the Canaries.
By T. L. Gent.

LONDON,
Imprinted by *Thomas Orwin* for *T.G.*
and *John Busbie.*
1590.

5

noted for this style, and it was he who first used the name *Euphues* as the title for his romantic novel, *Euphues, an Anatomy of Wit* (1578), followed by a sequel, *Euphues and his England* (1580). The style soon became fashionable in both literature and polite conversation in England, in the 16th and beginning of the 17th centuries. Shakespeare was well versed in euphuism, but he mocked it as much as he used it.

Just as Euphues means 'well-grown', Philautus has the connotation of 'Lover of fine, clean, elegant, splendid things', which goes well with the whole ethos of euphuism. The sons of Philautus are, therefore, those who love pure and refined things, and are themselves of this quality. According to the 'Schedule annexed to Euphues Testament', placed as a foreword to Lodge's *Rosalynde*, the mother of Philautus' sons is Camilla. Camilla was famed as a fierce warrior queen, queen of the Volsci, who was dedicated when young to the service of Diana, the divine huntress. Philautus and Camilla thus represent the Renaissance ideal and ethos of the scholar-warrior, epitomised in England by the character of Hemetes the Heremyte (*i.e.* Hermes the Hermit), who combined the qualities of Mars and Mercury, and person-ified by Sir Philip Sydney, the nation's hero.

The Schedule goes on to reveal that the 'sons' referred to are young but 'nobly born' and therefore with 'great minds'. Preceding the Schedule is Lodge's Letter, 'To the Gentlemen Readers', making it clear that Philautus' sons are gentlemen. Strictly speaking, *gentleman* was the term for a man of gentle birth (*ie* noble, or well-born), belonging to a family having both land and position, and entitled to bear arms. They were the so-called landed gentry, who ranged from the squires and knights up through the various levels of aristocracy. However, the term was also applied as the

complimentary designation of a member of certain societies
or professions, such as the gentlemen lawyers of the Inns of
Court, and of certain privileged students (the gentlemen
commoners) of the two universities, Oxford and
Cambridge. The euphuistic 'University Wits' were gentle-
men-poet-playwrights.

Another symbolic name is Silexedra, given as the
place where Euphues had his cell and where his golden
legacy, *Rosalynde*, was found. The cell is reminiscent of
the hermit's cave and Prospero's cell, and also of the cave
where the senior Duke and his friends found shelter in
the Forest of Arden. Silexedra is derived from the Latin,
silex, meaning 'crag, rock, cliff', and perhaps intentionally
makes a link to the famous crag, the Athenian acropolis,
where Pallas Athena, the great 'Spear-Shaker', had her
temple and capital. Alternatively, and perhaps even more
aptly, it might refer to the other famous crag or rocky
peak, Mount Parnassus,[6] the home of Athena and her
male counterpart Apollo. There also dwelt their 'sons',
Æsclepius, the great healer, and Dionysus (Bacchus), the
god of drama. Delphi is situated on the slopes of the
Parnassian mountain, together with its oracle and the
cave from which flows the Castalian spring of poetic
inspiration. Apollo and Athena are the classical archetypes (*i.e.* god and goddess) of poetry, philosophy and
illumination, and therefore of all philosopher-poets.[7] Both
Spenser[8] and Shakespeare[9] claimed that their muse was
Pallas Athena, and Shakespeare was further likened to
Apollo by Ben Jonson[10] and John Weaver.[11] Lodge, however, in humble vein, did not claim that his romance contained 'anie sprigs of Pallas bay tree', but 'some leaves of
Venus mirtle'.[12]

The main story of Lodge's *Rosalynde* is reused by
Shakespeare in a condensed form as the basis for his *As*

You Like It. Rosalynde's principal plot concerns the three sons of Sir John of Bordeaux, of whom the youngest son is mistreated by the eldest, and the adventures of the principal ladies, Rosalynde and Alinda, plus the subplot of the shepherds, Montanus, Phoebe and Corydon. The underlying plot deals with the usurpation of the throne by the bad King Torismond and the eventual restoration to the throne of the rightful King Gerismond. This restoration takes place by means of a battle and the slaying of the evil king.

Shakespeare converts the two kings to dukes and makes them brothers, and when the eventual restoration takes place, it is because the younger brother experiences a complete religious conversion, rather like Paul of Tarsus on the road to Damascus. However, the dukes and their daughters are referred to in the play in terms of royalty (*e.g.* 'your Highness', 'sovereign' and 'princess'), showing that Shakespeare still saw them as royal despite changing their titles.

The characters of Jaques, Audrey and Touchstone are introduced entirely new by Shakespeare, and the names of the other characters have been changed, except those of Rosalind (Rosalynde), Phebe (Phoebe), Adam and Charles the Wrestler. In addition, Shakespeare keeps the assumed names of the two ladies, Ganymede and Aliena, when in their disguise. He makes Celia leave her father to accompany her friend Rosalind out of love and free choice, whereas in Lodge's tale Alinda is banished by her father, King Torismond. Shakespeare adds the 'love-cure' offered by Rosalind to Orlando, the practical, down-to-earth and unromantic affair between Touchstone and Audrey, and the appearance of Hymen, the god of marriage, at the climax of the play.

There are allusions in *As You Like It* to contemporary works, such as Lyly's *The Woman in the Moon* (1597),

Marlowe's *Hero and Leander* (1598), Yonge's translation of Jorge de Montemayor's *Diana Enamorada* (1598) and Greene's *Orlando Furioso* (1599). Montemayor's *Diana*, which is referred to in *As You Like It* (IV, i, 146), was a major source of Renaissance pastoral romance, and it is not surprising that this was an important source for Shakespeare too.

The 'love-cure' proposed by Rosalind to Orlando in *As You Like It* in particular owes its origin to Lyly, or at least both playwrights used the same idea.[13] Greene's play, *The Historie of Orlando Furioso, one of the Twelve Peeres of France,* which was first performed *c.*1591, the same year that Sir John Harington's English translation of Ludovico Ariosto's *Orlando Furioso* was published, describes some of the same characteristics of Orlando as in Shakespeare's play. Shakespeare may have borrowed these characteristics from Greene's play, but the name of Orlando, as well as inspiration for Orlando's story, he probably obtained direct from Ariosto's epic poem. Italian literature—especially the works of Ariosto—were extremely fashionable in Elizabethan England, and Ariosto's *Orlando Furioso* (1532) and his play *I Suppositi* (1509) were an important literary source and inspiration for Shakespeare. Behind Ariosto's work lie the Classical sources of the Renaissance—in particular the Roman dramatists, Plautus and Terence, mentioned by Ariosto as his sources, and behind them are their even more ancient spring-heads.

Robert Greene (*c.*1560-1592) both knew and influenced Shakespeare, as did the other 'University Wits'—Thomas Lodge, John Lyly, Christopher Marlowe, George Peele and Thomas Nashe. Marlowe, who died in May 1593, is referred to directly by Phebe in *As You Like It,* who speaks a quotation from Marlowe's *Hero and Leander* ('Who ever lov'd that lov'd not at first sight?'), attributing it to a 'dead shepherd' (III, v, 81-2); whilst Rosalind comments on Marlowe's story in the following act (IV, i, 95-101). Since *Hero and Leander* was not published until 1598, Shakespeare must have read it in manuscript.

Further influences are derived from Sir Philip Sydney's pastoral romance, *Arcadia*, first published as *The Countess of Pembroke's Arcadia* in quarto in 1590 (Book 1 only) and in folio in 1593 (Books 1-4), and republished in folio in 1598. This 'heroic poesy', as C. S. Lewis put it, helped introduce romantic literature to England, combining romance with both heroic and pastoral (or naturalistic) themes, and complementing Edmund Spenser's *Shepheardes Calendar* (1579) and *Faerie Queene* (1590, 1598). Sir Philip was the brother of Mary, the Countess of Pembroke, to whose sons the Shakespeare 1st Folio was dedicated. She and her sons were, together with Essex and Southampton, patrons of the circle of poets and dramatists to which Shakespeare belonged. A number of Shakespeare's works, besides *As You Like It,* were directly inspired by Sidney's romance, such as *The Two Gentlemen of Verona* and the later 'Romances', *Pericles, Cymbeline, The Winter's Tale* and *The Tempest.* Spenser's works, likewise, were a great influence on Shakespeare.

The romantic comedies are like fairy tales: they all have 'happy ever after' endings. The theme of separation and reunion of family members and friends is important. So also is the theme of exile, with the banished characters—usually rulers or rulers-to-be—restored to their rightful homes and positions at the end of the play. The need for patience in adversity, the importance of providence in human affairs, and the hope of a better life, are major underlying themes. The main characters go on the hero's (or heroine's) journey, leaving a state of corruption and entering a wilderness or a place of natural beauty where lessons are learnt and the Wheel of Fortune spun around. Wrongs are redressed—the proud fall and the humble are raised—and, by means of love, all is brought to a higher, more harmonious and better state than at the beginning. All things culminate in a resolution, with love unions or marriages, feasts, revelations and joy.

The reason for this is that romantic literature is based on the Mysteries of Classical Greece and Rome, in which love is the force which drives people on to overcome all kinds of hardships and difficulties, as tests on the path of initiation. Such a driving force brings about heroism of the highest order: for love, not will or intellect, is the ultimate Law of the universe. This 'romanticism' was popularised by the Greek poet Theocritus (3rd century BC), whose *Idylls* were the first pastoral poems known as such. The *Eclogues* of the Latin poet Virgil (70-19 BC) were even more influential.

The Mysteries were the allegorical dramas, primarily of the pre-Christian Orphic Mystery schools of Greece and Rome, which people experienced as a means of learning about life and nature—divine, human and natural—and how to improve one's character and society as a whole. These Mysteries took place both in the temple precincts and in the wildness of nature, such as at Cumæ (near modern Naples in Italy) where the candidates for initiation, after a sea journey, had to descend into the cavernous depths of a mountain. Then, after a series of sorrowful experiences, they would find their way upwards and out into a hidden valley bathed in sunshine. There, in a 'golden' landscape of semi-wild beauty, they would experience the pastoral and romantic life before being led on further to the temple in the heights, where the mystical marriage and spiritual illumination took place.

It is in this context that the Masque of Hymen, celebrating the marriage of the lovers in *As You Like It*, should be understood: as an essential ingredient of the play that allows the immortals—the gods and goddesses—to enter the scene and be seen. This is in fact the Mystery—the vision seen by the mystics and experienced with full understanding by the epopts or seers. All Shakespeare's masques have this sacramental value: such as Jupiter on his eagle and the chanting ancestors in *Cymbeline*, the appearance of Diana in *Pericles,* the betrothal masque in *The Tempest*, and Queen Katharine's vision of angels in *Henry VIII.* Masque-like elements or simple maskings likewise occur in *The Winter's Tale* and earlier comedies such as *Love's Labour's Lost*, *Romeo and Juliet*, *Much Ado About Nothing* and *A Midsummer Night's Dream*. Masques are derived from the ancient Mysteries, particularly the Bacchanalias, in which the bacchants and bacchantes would mask themselves to represent (and embody, as in shamanism) the spirit of the gods and goddesses. Far from being spurious, masques were important to Shakespeare and clearly enjoyed by him, just as they were enjoyed by his contemporaries, the courtiers and nobility of the Royal Court and the gentlemen of the Inns of Court.

Not only were masques important to Shakespeare and part of his art, but so was music. Music was understood as related to the art of Orpheus, by means of which even the grossest of things and people could be inspired, healed and brought together in harmony—and this was the purpose of Shakespeare's art, using the combined music of poetry well spoken and song well sung. His later Romances make this purpose much clearer, although Jaques in *As You Like It* hints at the author's intentions in his well-known speech (II, vii, 42-61):

> *Jaques.*   O that I were a fool!
>> I am ambitious for a motley coat…..
>> Invest me in my motley. Give me leave
>> To speak my mind, and I will through and
>> through
>> Cleanse the foul body of th'infected world,
>> If they will patiently receive my medicine.

In *As You Like It* there are (or appear to be) more songs and music than in any other Shakespeare play:

1. 'Under the greenwood tree' - sung by Amiens, and concluded by Jaques (II, v).

2. 'Blow, blow, thou winter wind' – sung by Amiens (II, vii).

3. 'What shall he have that killed the deer?' – sung by two lords (IV, ii).

4. 'It was a lover and his lass' – sung by two pages (V, iii).[14]

5. *'Still music'* – played at the entrance of Hymen with Rosalind and Celia (V, iv).

6. The Wedlock Hymn – sung in honour of Hymen and marriage (V, iv).

7. Concluding wedding dance (end V, iv).

The music, the scintillating wit, the love poetry, the separations and exiling, the Arcadian 'wilderness' setting, the moral under and over-tones, the testing and transformation of the characters, the loves and hates, the heroism, the righting of wrongs, the redemption and illumination of the wicked, the marriages, and the reinstatement of the rightful duke in his position of responsibility—all testify to this play being not only a carefully formulated heroic romance but a Mystery play—not, perhaps, of the same order of greatness as Shakespeare's *Tempest,* with which it has affinities, but nevertheless a highly entertaining prototype.

2. The Story

Act 1, Scene 1—the Orchard of Oliver de Boys[15]

The play opens with Sir Rowland's third and youngest son, Orlando, reporting to his father's old and faithful servant, Adam, why he feels sad. The reason is that his eldest brother, Oliver, has ignored the will of their deceased father, Sir Rowland de Boys, which bequeathed Orlando a thousand crowns and charged Oliver with the good breeding of his youngest brother. Instead, Oliver keeps Jaques, the second brother, at school, but holds Orlando 'rustically at home', unkempt, without an education and treated like a peasant. Orlando expresses that this grieves him, and that the spirit of his father, which he believes is in him, 'begins to mutiny against this servitude'. He will no longer endure it, but doesn't know quite what he should do about it.

At that moment Oliver arrives and Orlando charges him with his maltreatment. Oliver strikes Orlando and Orlando responds by seizing him in a wrestler's grip. He refuses to let Oliver go until his elder brother promises to let him have some part of his inheritance. Oliver, however, once released, plots to revenge himself on Orlando and give him nothing.

Charles, the Duke's wrestling champion, arrives with news from the court, reporting the 'old' news that the old

15

Duke is banished by the new Duke, his younger brother who has usurped his older brother's place. Three or four loving lords have put themselves into voluntary exile with him. The younger brother, Duke Frederick, has taken advantage of this and confiscated their lands and revenues. The old Duke's daughter, Rosalind, however, is kept behind at court, being dearly loved by her cousin Celia, Duke Frederick's daughter, who would rather die than be parted from Rosalind. In reply to Oliver's question as to where the old Duke will live, Charles explains that he is already in the Forest of Arden, where he lives with many merry men like 'the old Robin Hood of England'. Moreover, many young gentlemen flock to him every day, and they 'fleet the time carelessly as they did in the golden world'.

Charles reveals that he has discovered that Orlando intends to challenge him, disguised, in the wrestling competition that is to take place the next day, but that he (Charles) is worried lest he might cause injury to the young man. Out of love he tells Oliver, so that Oliver might be able to find some way of dissuading his brother from the match or else be prepared for the disgrace such defeat might bring. Oliver, however, who already knows this secret, intends to use this as an opportunity to kill his brother, and so he asserts to Charles that Orlando is a secret villain who not only seeks his (Oliver's) life but will use any underhand means to slay Charles as well. Charles thus departs prepared to deal suitably with such a 'villain'.

The scene ends with Oliver musing on why his soul should hate nothing more than his youngest brother; yet his brother is gentle, learned without having had any schooling, full of noble device, and so beloved by many people of all kinds that he (Oliver) is 'altogether misprised'. He then departs to kindle Orlando's desire to wrestle Charles.

The Story

Act 1, Scene 2—before the Duke's Palace

Celia, Duke Frederick's daughter and only child, tries to cheer up her cousin, Rosalind, who is depressed over the banishment of her father. Celia pledges her love and friendship and loyalty. The two princesses try to make merry about falling in love and how to mock Fortune from her wheel, so that the goddess' gifts are bestowed more evenly. Touchstone, the court jester, arrives in the middle of the conversation, to call the princesses to the Duke, and jokes about the honour of a certain knight. Monsieur Le Beau, a courtier, arrives with news that the wrestler, Charles, has killed three men already in the wrestling competition, all three being the sons of an old man. The princesses are sad at this, but Le Beau continues by reporting that the competition is soon to be resumed on the very spot where they now stand.

As he says this, the Duke and his court arrive, together with Charles and Orlando. The Duke has tried to persuade Orlando not to fight, because of his youth. Rosalind and Celia, who take an immediate liking to Orlando when they see him, also speak to him to dissuade him from the match. However, Orlando is determined on the fight, explaining to the princesses that he has nothing left to lose or to live for. The match takes place and, to everyone's surprise, Orlando throws Charles and the defeated champion has to be carried away, leaving Orlando the victor. Duke Frederick asks Orlando what his name is; but, when Orlando reveals who he is, the Duke refuses to give him the prize, his reason being that Orlando's father stood against Frederick when he usurped the dukedom from his elder brother.

After the Duke and his court have left the scene, Celia and Rosalind remain behind. Celia is shocked at her father's treatment of Orlando, whilst Rosalind declares that her father loved Sir Rowland as his soul and, if she had known who Orlando was, she would have shed tears with her entreaties to him not to hazard his life so. They go to thank and encourage Orlando. Rosalind, who has already fallen in love with Orlando, gives him her chain from her neck to wear. As the princesses leave, Rosalind attempts further conversation with Orlando, but he is too tongue-tied to respond properly.

Le Beau returns and, out of friendship, advises Orlando to flee the place and the Duke's wrath. In answer to Orlando's queries, Le Beau explains that the smaller princess is Duke Frederick's daughter, whilst the other, the banished Duke's daughter, is detained by Duke Frederick in order to keep his daughter company. However, Le Beau reveals, Duke Frederick has taken displeasure against his niece because the people praise her for her virtues and pity her for her father's sake. He adds that he believes the Duke's malice against Rosalind will suddenly break forth. With this warning, Orlando thanks him and departs.

Act 1, Scene 3—the Duke's Palace

Just as Rosalind is telling Celia how much she has fallen in love with Orlando, Duke Frederick enters suddenly and in anger. Without any warning he banishes Rosalind from the court, charging her as a traitor because she is her father's daughter. Celia speaks up for Rosalind, with whom she has been brought up from childhood and from whom she has never been apart. She challenges her father's decision and declared motive, but he is resolute. He leaves the room, threatening death to Rosalind if she is not departed by the time given her. Celia then reaffirms her love for Rosalind and declares that she will flee with her friend, to seek Rosalind's father in the Forest of Arden.

Thinking of the possible dangers in the forest, they decide to disguise themselves—Celia as a peasant girl and Rosalind, because she is uncommonly tall, as her brother, bearing a cutlass and boar-spear. Rosalind's name is to be Ganymede and Celia's is to be Aliena. They also determine to ask Touchstone, the fool, to accompany them— who, Celia declares, would go 'o'er the wide world' with her. They leave the scene in order to gather their jewels and wealth, and to devise the fittest time and safest way to hide themselves from pursuit. Celia declares that they go 'to liberty, and not to banishment'.

Act 2, Scene 1—the Forest of Arden

In the Forest of Arden the banished Duke and his noblemen discuss the pleasures of life in the forest, noting that, despite the challenges of nature, the natural life is more free from peril than the envious and corrupt court, and teaches them about goodness. One of the lords reports how he and Amiens came upon their companion, the melancholy Jaques, lying under an oak, lamenting the mortal injury of a deer that had just been shot. The Duke expresses a wish to join him immediately, remarking that Jaques is 'full of matter' when in such a sullen fit.

Act 2, Scene 2—The Duke's Palace

Discovering that the princesses have fled, Duke Frederick tries to discover whether anyone saw them go. He is told that Hisperia, a gentlewoman of one of the princesses, secretly overheard the two princesses admiring the young wrestler who defeated Charles, and that she believes they will be wherever he is. The Duke orders his attendants to go to Oliver's house, and if they cannot find Orlando there, then they are to arrest his brother, whom the Duke will use to find the 'foolish runaways'.

Act 2, Scene 3—before Oliver's House

Adam finds Orlando and warns him not to enter the house, for his brother Oliver means to kill him. Orlando replies that he does not wish to be forced to live his life as a highway robber and would rather face his brother, but Adam entreats him to flee and offers to give Orlando all the gold—five hundred crowns—that he has saved for his old age. He declares that, despite his age, he is fit and strong, and asks to be Orlando's servant in his exile. Orlando gratefully accepts and they leave together.

Act 2, Scene 4—the Forest of Arden

Rosalind (disguised as Ganymede), Celia (disguised as Aliena, Ganymede's sister) and Touchstone, weary with travel, arrive at last in the Forest of Arden. They encounter an old man (Corin), a shepherd, walking with a youth and engaged in conversation. The young man (Silvius) speaks of being madly in love with Phebe, a shepherdess. After Silvius has left the old man and run on ahead, the three runaways approach Corin to see if they can buy some food. They discover from him that his master, who owns the flock, the pasture and a cottage, has put them up for sale. Ganymede (Rosalind) and Aliena (Celia) decide to buy them and ask the old shepherd to arrange the purchase and then to work for them, which he gladly agrees to do.

The Story

Act 2, Scene 5—the Forest of Arden

Lord Amiens, Jaques and others assemble in another part of the forest to prepare a picnic for the Duke, who is yet to arrive. Amiens begins singing a ballad, 'Under the greenwood tree,' about the sweet but austere life in the forest, open to the weather. Jaques, in melancholic vein, joins in with additional verses of his own, mocking those who have voluntarily joined the Duke in exile and lost their lands in the process.

Act 2, Scene 6—the Forest of Arden

Orlando and Adam have arrived in Arden. Adam collapses on the ground, exhausted and thinking himself dying of hunger. Orlando, at first determined to go in search of food for Adam, realises that the air is too bleak where he is and decides to carry Adam to where there might be shelter, and then to find some food.

Act 2, Scene 7—the Forest of Arden

The old Duke and his followers are eating their picnic, but missing Jaques. Then Jaques appears, reporting excitedly that he has met a court fool in the forest, who moralised on time. Jaques is quite taken with the fool and wishes to be one himself, so as to have the liberty of being able to satirise without fear of reprisal, and thereby 'cleanse the foul body of th'infected world'. The Duke comments sourly that, because Jaques has led the life of a sensual libertine, he is more likely to spread disease than do good. Jaques (who had been made a bankrupt) replies with a tirade against pride, luxury, and the costly, ostentatious fashions of city women that can over-tax any private person.

Orlando comes upon them and rushes into their presence with sword drawn, demanding food. The Duke, instead of reacting with like force, invites Orlando to join them in their feast. Orlando apologises for his rude behaviour and asks if they will wait for him to return with an 'old poor man, who after me hath limp'd in pure love'. Whilst Orlando is gone to fetch Adam, the Duke observes to his followers that they are not all alone in their unhappy state. Jaques soliloquises on how all the world is a stage, and enumerates, melancholically, the seven ages of man. By the time he has finished, Orlando returns with Adam. They all set to and eat whilst Amiens sings. The Duke expresses how pleased he is to welcome Orlando as good Sir Rowland's son, and Adam with him.

Act 3, Scene 1—the Duke's Palace

Duke Frederick, interrogating Oliver, does not believe Oliver's denial of having seen Orlando since the wrestling match and flight of his daughter and niece. He charges Oliver, under threat of banishment, with finding Orlando within the year and bringing the runaway, dead or alive, to the Duke. In the meantime the Duke seizes all Oliver's lands and possessions, as surety.

Act 3, Scene 2—the Forest of Arden

Orlando wanders through the forest, hanging love poems to Rosalind on the trees and carving her name into the bark. Corin and Touchstone walk together, the fool baiting the old shepherd concerning his simple life and lack of courtly manners. Corin, however, is unabashed and unashamed at his shepherd's life. They come upon Ganymede (Rosalind), who is reading out loud one of the love poems that 'he' has found on a tree. Touchstone, reading another verse, makes mockery of them. Then Aliena (Celia) joins them, reading another poem. She dismisses Touchstone and Corin. Conversing privately with Rosalind, Celia asks Rosalind whether she realises who has written the poems. She teasingly reveals to her friend that the love-struck poet is Orlando, whom she found by accident under an oak tree.

At that moment Orlando and Jaques enter, and the women eavesdrop on their conversation. The men banter about the love poetry, Jaques requesting that Orlando mar no more trees with his love-songs and Orlando asking Jaques not to mar his verses by reading them. Jaques mocks Orlando for his love and Orlando chides Jaques for his critical and melancholic mind. They part company, with Jaques leaving and Orlando remaining. Rosalind, as Ganymede, approaches Orlando and plays a game of witticism with him about time. Then she offers to cure him of his lovesickness, the cure being that she (Ganymede) should woo him every day as if she (Ganymede) were Rosalind, whilst she would act as if she were that lady and soon put him off his love by her changeable and difficult nature. Orlando, eager to be cured, agrees to this.

Act 3, Scene 3—the Forest of Arden

Jaques witnesses Touchstone wooing Audrey, a goatherd, who consents to marry the court jester in the woods. Touchstone has already organised a priest, Sir Oliver Martext, to take the service, and Sir Oliver arrives ready for the marriage. However, Sir Oliver insists that the bride must have someone to give her away. Jaques steps forward to play the role, but objects at the irregularity of the arrangements. He persuades Touchstone to follow him with Audrey, to find either a church or a more appropriate manner in which to be married.

Act 3, Scene 4—the Forest of Arden

(The following morning) Rosalind is upset and weeps that Orlando is late for his promised rendezvous. Celia tries to comfort her. During the conversation Rosalind mentions that on the previous day she met the Duke her father, although he did not recognise her (he was banished when Rosalind was still a child).[16] Corin the shepherd enters and invites them to witness the courtship of Phebe by Silvius, in whom they have taken an interest.

Act 3, Scene 5—the Forest of Arden

Safely concealed, Rosalind, Celia and Corin eavesdrop on Silvius' wooing of Phebe. Phebe, however, rejects Silvius' advances with scorn. Rosalind, angry at such treatment of a lover, intercedes and castigates Phebe for disdaining someone who loves her so well. Still disguised as Ganymede, she points out to Phebe that she is not beautiful and therefore not for all markets, and that therefore she should accept what is on offer. Embarrassingly for Rosalind, Phebe falls instantly in love with her as Ganymede. When the ladies are gone, Phebe asks Silvius to act as a messenger for her to Ganymede, to whom she intends to write.

Act 4, Scene 1—the Forest of Arden

Meanwhile, Jaques finds Rosalind (Ganymede) in order to become better acquainted with the 'pretty youth'. They begin by discussing melancholy, which Jaques loves. Rosalind, however, says that she would rather have a fool to make her merry than experience to make her sad, and derides Jaques for selling his lands simply to have such sad experience. When Orlando finally arrives, Jaques leaves and Rosalind (as Ganymede) berates Orlando for being late. They begin the 'love-cure', with Rosalind, as Ganymede, posing as Rosalind, satirising Orlando's talk of love. Rosalind (Ganymede) asks Celia (Aliena) to perform the priest's role in a mock marriage between them, then warns Orlando as to how wayward a wise wife might be.

Orlando, announcing that he has to leave for two hours in order to attend the Duke at dinner, gets up to leave. Rosalind makes him promise to return on time, at two o'clock. When he has gone, Celia castigates Rosalind for misusing the female sex in her 'love-prate', but Rosalind confesses that Celia simply cannot know how deep she is in love with Orlando.

Act 4, Scene 2—the Forest of Arden

Jaques and the lords are hunting in the forest and a deer has been killed. Jaques proposes that the lord who killed the stag should be presented to the Duke like a Roman conqueror, with the deer's horns upon his head. He proposes that a song should be sung, and without more ado the hunters set to with singing.

Act 4, Scene 3—the Forest of Arden

To Rosalind's dismay, Orlando is late again for his tryst. Silvius appears, bearing a letter from Phebe for Ganymede. Still disguised as Ganymede, Rosalind mocks both its contents and Phebe, then reads the letter out aloud for Silvius to hear, hoping to make him realise the falseness of the woman he loves. Seeing a man approaching, she sends Silvius away with an answer to Phebe, that she should love Silvius.

The man who arrives is Oliver, who enquires the way to the 'sheep-cote fenced about with olive-trees'. But then he realises that he has found the couple for whom he is looking. He reports that Orlando commends himself to them both and has given him a bloody napkin to present to 'that youth he calls his Rosalind'. Oliver than explains how Orlando, wandering through the forest, had come upon 'a wretched ragged man' sleeping on his back. A poisonous snake had wrapped itself about his neck and was about to strike the man's mouth when, seeing Orlando, it rapidly unwound itself and slipped away into a bush. In the shade of the bush, Orlando perceived a hungry lioness waiting to pounce upon the man as soon as he should stir. Realising that the sleeping man was his eldest brother, Orlando twice was tempted to leave him to his fate, but natural kindness overcame these thoughts and he gave battle to the lioness, who quickly fell before him.

Oliver then reveals that he was the slumbering man whose life was saved by his brother Orlando. He explains that he is not now the same man, in that he has undergone a conversion. Rosalind is anxious about the meaning of the bloody napkin. Oliver describes how Orlando led him to the Duke, who gave him fresh clothes and food; but then how, when Orlando stripped, a great gash was revealed upon his arm where the lioness had torn some flesh away. When Orlando fainted from loss of blood, crying upon Rosalind, Oliver bound up the wound. Then, when Orlando had recovered sufficient strength, he sent Oliver to find Ganymede so as to tell his story and give the youth the bloody napkin.

Rosalind faints at this report. Reviving, and still pretending to be Ganymede, she tries to explain her faint as a counterfeit and asks Oliver to report as much to Orlando.

Act 5, Scene 1—the Forest of Arden

Touchstone and Audrey are making their way through the forest when they encounter William, who is also a suitor of hers. Touchstone makes fun of the untutored man and then threatens him with dire consequences if he does not relinquish his suit. Touchstone explains that he is the one who will marry Audrey, and Audrey confirms that it is better that William leaves—which he immediately does. Corin appears, to summon the couple to their 'master' and mistress.

Act 5, Scene 2—the Forest of Arden

Orlando and Oliver are together discussing the amazing fact that Oliver has fallen in love with Aliena at first sight, and she with him, and that they have both agreed to marry each other. Oliver affirms that this is definitely so, and that he is willing to surrender to Orlando the house and all the revenue that was bequeathed him by their father, whilst he will remain in Arden with Aliena, to live and die a shepherd. Orlando readily gives his assent to the wedding taking place on the morrow, to which he will invite the Duke and all his followers.

Oliver takes his leave as Ganymede (Rosalind) appears. Ganymede further confirms how suddenly passionate and resolute in love are 'his' sister and Oliver. Orlando confesses how bitter a thing it is to look into happiness through another man's eyes, and that he longs for Rosalind. He can no longer live by thinking. Rosalind, whom Orlando still believes is Ganymede, responds to this appeal by claiming that ever since 'he' was three years old 'he' has learnt magic from a great magician, practised in the good arts, not evil; and that if Orlando really does love Rosalind as much as he claims, then when his brother Oliver marries Aliena he (Orlando) shall marry Rosalind.

At that moment Silvius and Phebe come upon them. Phebe is upset that Ganymede should have shown her letter to Silvius. Ganymede replies that it was done intentionally, for she (Phebe) should learn to love faithful Silvius. Ganymede promises Phebe that 'he' would love her if 'he' could, and that on the morrow 'he' will marry Phebe if 'he' should ever marry a woman. Ganymede promises Orlando that 'he' will satisfy him tomorrow, and Silvius that he (Silvius) will be married tomorrow. Charging them to meet the next day for these purposes, they all agree not to fail.

Act 5, Scene 3—the Forest of Arden

Touchstone announces to Audrey that tomorrow they shall be married. Audrey responds, saying that she desires it with all her heart. Two pages arrive, and Touchstone asks them to sing a song. They sing, 'It was a lover and his lass'.

Act 5, Scene 4—the Forest of Arden

The 'morrow' has arrived and the Duke and his attendant

lords assemble for the magic and the marriages. Orlando confides that he is unsure that the magic will work, but he hopes it will. Rosalind, still disguised as Ganymede, joins them. She begins by eliciting promises from the Duke that he will bestow his daughter in marriage upon Orlando, and from Orlando that he will have Rosalind as his wife if Ganymede can bring her there. Ganymede (Rosalind) then asks Phebe that, if she should after all refuse to marry him, she will give herself instead to Silvius—to which request Phebe agrees. Silvius likewise agrees to have Phebe, 'though to have her and death were both one thing'.

Ganymede then announces that 'he' has promised to make all this matter even, Exhorting them each to keep their promises, 'he' leaves them temporarily. Whilst Ganymede is away, the Duke mentions that 'this shepherd boy' reminds him of 'some lively touches' of his daughter. Orlando, supporting this, confesses that from the very first he thought Ganymede must be a brother to Rosalind; but he dismisses this idea, excusing it as a result of Ganymede being tutored in magic by a great magician who is 'obscured in the circle of this forest'.

Touchstone and Audrey arrive. After an amusing interlude in which Jaques is able to show the Duke what a witty fool Touchstone is, music begins to sound. Into the assembled company appears Hymen, the god of marriage, accompanied by Rosalind and Celia, as themselves. Hymen announces that there is mirth in heaven when earthly things, made even, atone together. The god presents the Duke with his daughter, so that the Duke might join her hand in marriage with Orlando. Rosalind gives herself to her father, as his daughter, and then to Orlando, as his wife. The men realise that this is truly Rosalind. Phebe realises she has been mistaken and bids her love 'adieu'.

Hymen breaks in on the bewildered amazement, stating that he must 'bar confusion' and 'make conclusion of these most strange events'. The god brings the eight lovers together to join hands and make four married couples. A wedlock hymn is then sung to celebrate the marriages and to allow time for the participants to feed themselves with questioning, so that reason may diminish their wonder concerning how they first met and how these things finish.

As they celebrate, and the Duke welcomes his niece as well as his daughter, Jaques de Boys arrives on the scene. He asks for audience and announces that he is the second son of old Sir Rowland. He brings news that Duke Frederick, having heard how every day men of great worth join the exiled Duke in the forest, had raised an army in order to fight and kill his brother. However, when he arrived at the edge of the forest, he met with an old religious man and, after some questioning together, Duke Frederick was converted not only from pursuing his enterprise to fight and kill his brother but also from all worldly matters. He intended to seek a religious life; and so, dying to the world, he bequeathed his crown to his banished brother and restored all confiscated lands to those in exile with the good Duke.

The Duke calls on everyone to complete the celebration of the marriages, after which he will share his fortune with all, 'according to the measure of their states', and return to court to rule in his rightful place. Jaques, however, decides to join Duke Frederick, to hear and learn more.

The play concludes with dancing, after which Rosalind is left alone to speak the epilogue, emphasising that it is just as appropriate to see the lady as the epilogue as to see the lord as the prologue, and asserting that, as a magician, her way is to conjure us all, for the love we bear each other, to like as much of the play as pleases us.

3. Plots & Themes

The Main Plot

As You Like It is a play rich in plots, some of which are, from dramatic necessity, somewhat abridged. One main plot, however, stands out above the rest and provides the hero and heroine who are the real driving force and exoteric *raison d'être* of the play. This is the love story of Orlando and Rosalind.

Orlando and Rosalind fall in love with each other at first sight. Both are exiled from their homes, with their lives threatened, and both have to live as virtual outlaws in the forest. There they make their new homes and do good deeds. There they meet each other again and, after some disguise and play-acting on Rosalind's part, they marry. The fact that they accomplish all this, together with the manner in which they do it, seems to be the principal factor that initiates and resolves matters for everyone else.

The story of Orlando appears to be borrowed from the fairy tale of Cinderella, only with the sexes reversed. He is the youngest of three sons of a father who has died. Unlike Cinderella, he does not have a mother who is still alive, which would be the reverse equivalent to the Cinderella story. However, Orlando does have an elder brother (the eldest son) who is responsible for his upbringing and who treats him badly. Like Cinderella, Orlando is kept like an unpaid servant, but whereas Cinderella is forced to sleep in the cinders of the fireplace (hence her name), all that we know about Orlando is that he is made to eat with the servants and denied any kind of education or training. Orlando moans that his treatment 'differs not from the stalling of an ox' and that Oliver's 'horses are bred better' (I, i, 9-11).

Unlike Cinderella's second sister, who participates in the maltreatment of Cinderella, Orlando's middle brother Jaques is kept away at school, and 'report speaks goldenly of his profit' (I, i, 5-6). Nevertheless, as in the Cinderella story, Orlando meets his princess. Instead of a ball, however, the meeting takes place at a wrestling match, where the princess has a chance to see Orlando's strong, half-naked body in action and fall in love with his Herculean character and bravery—a fitting counterpart to the beautifully attired and graceful dancing 'princess' whom the prince fell in love with at the royal ball. The flight of Orlando after the wrestling match is due to the anger and evil intentions of the usurping duke rather than the magical transformation of a ball dress into rags and a coach into a pumpkin, but the effect is the same. Unlike Cinderella's prince, Orlando's princess is banished by a more powerful uncle and has to flee into the wilderness. However, as in the fairy tale, the hero and heroine find each other again, although it is by means of love verses hung on trees rather than by means of a fancy slipper. They marry and, to all intents and purposes, 'live happily ever after'.

Orlando embarks on a typical hero's journey. He finds his love (briefly), is separated from her, undergoes a life-threatening challenge in which he rescues someone from death, meets his love again, wins her anew and is married to her.

Likewise, Rosalind dances the heroine's path. She is separated from her father, then from her love as soon as she has met him, and finally from her home and family comforts. She is compelled to endure danger and use her wits. She has to demonstrate love in a selfless way, like the hero but from a woman's point of view. She finds and wins her man, and is married to him. In doing this she takes on a man's disguise, although she is never a man: her strength and courage, initiative and cunning—and especially her magic—are all her own.

The Three Sub-Plots

Complementing the main plot of Rosalind and Orlando are three subsidiary plots, all of which concern love affairs that culminate in marriage. These are the three love stories of Oliver and Celia, Touchstone and Audrey, and Silvius and Phebe.

Celia accompanies Rosalind. Hers is also a heroine's journey, sacrificing all for love of her childhood friend, and eventually meeting and marrying Oliver, her romantic love. His is a transformational journey, ridding himself from his initial malice and bringing out his better character. It cannot exactly be said that he is a hero, but he becomes what Celia loves. Hence, as occurred with Orlando and Rosalind, 'They no sooner looked than they loved' (V, ii, 33-34).

The love affair of Touchstone and Audrey is an interesting 'reverse' parallel; for in this story we have an 'allowed' (*i.e.* professional) fool who also gives up a great deal in order to accompany his dear young mistress into danger and exile. His romantic love, Audrey, has a simplicity that is honest and innocent, not culpable like the women of the city such as those upon whom Jaques once squandered his time and wealth. She is a goatherd, whose position is virtually at the bottom of the social hierarchy, whom Touchstone calls 'a poor virgin, sir, an ill-favoured thing, sir, but all mine own' (V, iv, 57-58). This is a heart-touching affair—or, as Touchstone also hints, an entirely practical arrangement to meet certain basic needs, depending on how one takes it. However, Touchstone does say, enigmatically and from the heart, that it is 'a poor humour of mine sir, to take that that no man else will' (V, iv, 58-59).

For all the word play, Touchstone is no fool in the sense of being stupid, and his implied lasciviousness may not be much different from the sexuality of the other couples, which quite naturally plays a substantial part in their mutual attraction for each other. (Oliver and Celia, for instance, are described as being 'in the very wrath of love' - V, ii, 39.) The allowed fool is ready and willing to marry his virgin goatherd before witnesses and to live with her in the forest, becoming a goatherd himself. How long this marriage might last, we can only guess, but he does give up the possibility of continuing and probably enlarging a privileged life-style, that others might envy, for an alter-native that is remarkably rough and basic. In doing so, it is possible that Touchstone might release his love from her dark ignorance and baseness to one of more light and grace, whilst she might give him the true, faithful love and sincerity for which he longs. He gives a hint that he sees a real treasure that he values, in the heart of Audrey, when he says to Duke Senior concerning her: 'Rich honesty dwells like a miser sir, in a poor house, as your pearl in your foul oyster' (V, iv, 60-61). Touchstone may indeed be a disguised hero and Audrey a veiled pearl of great price.

Silvius and Phebe have another kind of relationship, but again it has its parallels with those of the other couples.

Silvius is, in his simple way, entirely faithful in his love and ever willing to serve Phebe. She takes advantage of this, whilst at the same time scorning him. However, at the end, her self-pride takes a fall and she is ready and willing to keep her word and marry her faithful lover. He, on his part, will take her, 'though to have her and death were both one thing' (v, iv, 17). He is a hero of a kind, and Phebe, rather than eat her word, prefers to keep it (v, iv, 148).

The Three Supporting Plots

Supporting the main plot and three sub-plots are three further stories, those of Jaques the melancholic, Touchstone the fool, and Adam the servant.

These three represent three classes of society: Jaques the gentleman, Adam the servant, and Touchstone the fool, who belongs to the class of professional artists (along with farmers and merchants) that lies midway between the class status of other two. All three, however, share one thing in common: they each give up material things for something finer. In another poet's words, they put their hands into the hand of God and step out into the dark unknown. Jaques gives up his old licentious life and sells his estates to go in search of knowledge. Adam gives up his life's savings, home and job to help Orlando and to accompany him as his servant. Touchstone leaves court, and his position and favour there, to accompany his young mistress, Celia. They all go as exiles to the forest.

Background Plot

All these, however, are but the foreground stories that take place against a background drama of some intensity and power. This background drama is that of the two brother dukes.

Like Prospero in Shakespeare's *Tempest*, the eldest brother and rightful duke has his position usurped by his younger brother and is banished—cast adrift, as it were, on a sea of dangerous fortune. Like Prospero, he finds a home, a forest rather than an island, but just the same in terms of being exiled and outlawed. Also like Prospero, in this wilderness of nature he sets up home in a cave. Like Prospero, he has a daughter who is his only child and heir; but, unlike the magus of *The Tempest,* he is separated from his daughter and does not have her with him in exile. Yet he is not alone, for many friends flock to him, to share his predicament.

Whilst in the forest, the banished Duke learns good things from nature: 'And this our life, exempt from public haunt, finds tongues in trees, books in the running brooks, sermons in stones, and good in everything' (II, i, 15-18). Moreover, the wild elements of nature teach him about himself: 'These are counsellors that feelingly persuade me what I am' (II, i, 10-11).

If the analogy with Prospero is anything to go by, and this is a theme with Shakespeare, then the good Duke may well have been usurped because he neglected his duties of state, by reason of a passion for studying books and meditating in prayer. Whilst living in the wild, he redresses the balance by learning from the experiences that nature alone gives, just as Prospero does on his island.

Eventually, the Duke is released from his exile by the conversion and repentance of his brother, which takes place 'on the skirts of this wild forest' (V, iv, 158). Prospero's brother, Antonio, likewise has to leave Milan and enter the wilderness of nature in order for the transformations to occur, although whether Antonio is actually converted to a more friendly way of life is left to our imagination to decide. However, the elder Duke in *As You Like It*, like Prospero in *The Tempest*, is able to return home and take up his rightful position once again—but, of course, with a difference. This time, thanks to his experiences in nature, he is a better man than before and potentially a far better ruler of his dukedom. Not only that, but many problems that used to exist have now been resolved and transmuted to a finer state of affairs, and there is a harmony and joy that was not there previously.

As for the younger brother, Duke Frederick, from being a violent, ambitious and corrupt man of the world he transforms into someone who gives up all worldly goods and passions, seeking instead a religious life. He, too, was unbalanced like his brother, but unlike his brother he was off-centre in the opposite, materialistic way. By the end of the play he makes a start at redressing this balance. The older Duke has already taken this step, so in this sense he is one or maybe two steps ahead of Frederick—but then, he is older, and there wouldn't be an *As You Like It* story otherwise!

Themes

Love & Hate

It could be said that all Shakespeare's plays contain the same great theme, which is that of love contrasted with its opposites, such as hate. This is the great theme of the Classical Mysteries, discussed by philosophers and taught by prophets, priests and priestesses down the ages. They also teach that all manifestation occurs because of polarity, and that when the opposites are resolved again into their union then all will vanish into their source. A hint of this is given by Shakespeare in the famous lines spoken by Prospero in *The Tempest*:

> *Prospero*……….. …………..Be cheerful, sir.
> Our revels now are ended. These our actors,
> As I foretold you, were all spirits, and
> Are melted into air, into thin air:
> And like the baseless fabric of this vision,
> The cloud-capp'd towers, the gorgeous palaces,
> The solemn temples, the great globe itself,
> Yea, all which it inherit, shall dissolve,
> And, like this insubstantial pageant faded,
> Leave not a rack behind. We are such stuff
> As dreams are made on; and our little life
> Is rounded with a sleep.[17]

The greatest description of this mystery, however, is given in Shakespeare's beautiful love poem, *The Phoenix and Turtle*. For it is by love that everything is created and in love that everything is resolved: first into a harmony, then a beauty, then a joy of union—a mystical marriage and 'mutual flame' of love:

> So they lov'd, as love in twain
> Had the essence but in one:
> Two distincts, division none;
> Number there in love was slain.[18]

The Orphic philosophers summed up their teachings by explaining that Love is the great gravitating or attracting force which brought the universe into shape and gave birth to the starry spheres, out of chaos. However, its opposite power is necessary to prevent everything unifying or marrying, and thus becoming one universal light, until the purpose of evolution is fulfilled. The purpose of evolution is to know God. Put another way, Unity, whilst it separates itself from itself, identifies itself. When differences resolve into their source or unity, so do they cease to exist.

The source is love: unity is love. Hate only exists temporarily as an aberration or difference which will eventually vanish, just as it does in *As You Like It* with the sudden conversion of both Oliver and Duke Frederick. These are the two main characters who manifest hate: Oliver for his youngest brother, Orlando, and Frederick for his elder brother, the rightful Duke. Frederick then extends his hate and jealousy to Orlando and Rosalind.

By contrast, those who demonstrate the greatest love are Orlando, Rosalind, Celia, Touchstone and Adam. Although not so prominent in the play, the elder Duke also shows great love, and so is described as the 'good Duke', loved by many for his quality of goodness. Such goodness is the greatest of all virtues:

> I take Goodness in this sense, the affecting of the weal of men, which is that the Grecians used to call *Philanthropia*; and the word *humanity* (as it is used) is a little too light to express it. Goodness I call the habit, and Goodness of Nature the inclination. This of all virtues and dignities of the mind is the greatest; being the character of the Deity: and without it man is a busy, mischievous, wretched thing; no better than a kind of vermin. Goodness answers to the theological virtue Charity.....[19]

Innocence & Corruption

Hand in hand with the theme of love and hate is that of corruption and innocence. The corruption is associated with the city, and the innocence or purity of life with the natural environment of the forest. The former is a man-made environment, whilst the latter is nature's own, made by God. However, although easy to say, these statements are not quite true. Mankind is also made by God and cities are built on natural sites, whilst the Forest of Arden is partly cultivated, with groves of olive trees and pastures for domesticated sheep and goats. Moreover, corruption and innocence exist in both places. In fact, what is really contrasted in the play is the culture of the city as compared to the culture of the forest, and the various motives and behaviour of the different people in the different places.

At first sight, the forest life or culture is portrayed as being innocent and free of any corrupting influences. It is not idyllic, however, and the characters who live there, either in exile or as peasants, make it clear that life is both rough and tough. In addition, the forest has its dangers, howbeit of a different kind to those of the city. The elder Duke is the first to describe the purity of the forest, asking his followers: 'Hath not old custom made this life more sweet than that of painted pomp? Are not these woods more free from peril than the envious court?' (II, i, 2-4). Audrey, the goatherd, seems to sum up the honesty of the forest life, for which Touchstone is seeking. Yet, at the same time, the forest is home to people like Phebe, who is dishonest to whomsoever she pleases; and Touchstone points out to the shepherd, Corin, that even shepherds interfere with the course of nature and make animals breed unnaturally and painfully for man's own gain (III, ii, 76-84). Moreover, we discover that the Duke is actually unhappy living in exile in the forest, despite the valuable education that it gives (II, vii, 136), and he and his followers return to the city as soon as they can.

Good and Evil

Shakespeare, therefore, gives us plenty of food for thought concerning what is corrupt and what is pure, what is good and what is evil. It is not a simple case of this is black and that is white: all things are mixed—but good can and does come out of bad, which is perhaps the major theme and lesson of the play. Not for nothing, therefore, does the play begin with Orlando in the orchard with Adam, reminding us of the original Garden of Eden and the Tree of Knowledge of Good and Evil.

The possibility of good coming out of evil, of a person's character changing from corrupt to virtuous, is portrayed dramatically by both Duke Frederick and Oliver. Both men become transformed by the experiences. Both provide examples of what Plato referred to as the only true birth: that of the spiritual soul of man rising out of the womb of his fleshly nature.

There is also one other prime example of this process, which is that of the elder Duke. One might not say that he comes from a condition of evil—as far as we know that is not true, as he is described as 'good'—but he does transform from a position of weakness to one of strength. His weakness, however, could be described as an evil, although not a personal one, for any weakness or imbalance in one's character and life can affect others detrimentally and allow evil to flourish. When one is a duke, responsible for the welfare of thousands of people and vast areas of land, such weaknesses can become magnified many times over and affect a whole society.

Love & Melancholy

As in the above example, not all things are evil. Life is fundamentally good, for it is of God, the All-Good; and life has many times been equated with love by the great teachers of humanity. Life manifests through polarity, and there are polarities within all things, none of which need be evil. For instance, we only see things through the interplay of light and dark. If all was light, or all was dark, we would see nothing. We both see and think by comparisons, and we are able to move because the ground under our feet remains relatively still. All knowledge is derived from the experience and comparison of opposites.

One of these great comparisons which Shakespeare uses in many of his plays is that of love and melancholy. Love is equated with light and melancholy with darkness. The kind of love being referred to in this comparison is that of mercy or compassion, which is generous, kind and dispassionate. Merciful love is represented traditionally by the 'planet' Jupiter, with all that that means—*e.g.* joviality, kindness, generosity, wisdom. (*N.B.* passionate love is symbolised by Venus.)

Whereas love is of the heart, melancholy is of the mind. Except it be illuminated by the light of love shining from the heart like a sun, the mind remains dark and cold. However, because the mind is naturally dark, when the light does shine in the darkness, the mind can see it and know it. This darkness of the mind is equated with melancholy, for it is the nature of the mind to want to see and know, which nature is called melancholy. Until it sees and knows, the mind is dark. When the mind becomes illumined, the melancholy transforms into knowledge. The traditional symbol for both melancholy and knowledge is Saturn, which is the natural counterpart or polarity to Jupiter. The two go together.

In *As You Like It,* the jovial, loving nature is strongly represented by Rosalind, and the saturnine, melancholic nature by Jaques. Rosalind has a great responsiveness and commitment to love and life. She enters fully into her experiences, whether of the court or of the forest, with vivacity, warmth, generosity of heart and commitment. In contrast to this, Jaques voluntarily withdraws from the complexities and responsibilities of life, in order to study life through observing other people's experiences. Whilst Rosalind is actively kind and helpful to others, Jaques is cool and critical. She is optimistic, he is pessimistic. She loves to laugh and be happy, he loves to be sad and say nothing. They both have their parts to play, but in the end Rosalind shows up Jaques' type of melancholy to be both costly to maintain and of little worth to the world at large (IV, i, 1-28):

> *Jaques.* ...It is a melancholy of mine own, compounded of many simples, extracted from many objects, and indeed the sundry contemplation of my travels, in which my rumination wraps me in most humorous sadness.
>
> *Ros.* A traveller! By my faith, you have great reason to be sad. I fear you have sold your own lands to see other men's. Then to have seen much and to have nothing is to have rich eyes and poor hands.
>
> *Jaques.* Yes, I have gained my experience.
>
> *Ros.* And your experience makes you sad. I had rather have a fool to make me merry than experience to make me sad, and to travel for it too!

Rosalind's love is Orlando, who also plays a jovial part. He is her counterpart or polarity in an entirely different way to Jaques. He expresses himself with writing love-songs, which Jaques reads 'ill-favouredly'. He loves Rosalind and loves her name, which he both speaks and writes often, but Jaques simply dislikes Rosalind's name, thereby coolly dismissing her who carries it as if of no account. In this Jaques is not stupid but cynical, for the love poetry is a courtly affectation that was in vogue at the time, which Shakespeare satirises whilst not condemning it entirely, and Orlando is so in love with Rosalind's name that he fails to recognise her under another name, Ganymede. But Jaques does not recognise her either, and cynicism is not a kind or helpful thing to others. Moreover, Orlando enjoys company, but Jaques prefers to be alone—although he hangs on to other people, like a shadow, and uses them and their experiences to gain knowledge for himself. In the end, Orlando gets the better of Jaques' bitterness and is able to get rid of the sad 'fool' (III, ii, 248-289).

Generosity & Martialness

Another polarity which often appears in life, and of which Shakespeare makes regular use, is the contrast between the generous and the martial natures. Generosity likes to share, whilst martialism takes for itself. Generosity is peaceful, martialism is aggressive. Generosity, when given with true love and wisdom, hurts none, but martialism often hurts, although it can also protect. These two natures are represented in the Neoplatonic Wisdom tradition by Jupiter and Mars. Both can be good features of life and both are essential to life, as polarities to each other.

A dramatic example of this polarity in *As You Like It* occurs during the picnic scene in the forest (II, vii, 88-135). Orlando, in desperation, bursts in upon the picnic with sword drawn, demanding food. The Duke, however, quietly invites him to dine with the whole company and to have whatever he wishes. Just as love and joviality will always reign supreme over sad melancholy, so loving generosity will melt the armour of the warrior. Orlando is naturally disarmed. He apologises for his martial behaviour and accepts the Duke's hospitality.

The Renaissance ideal of the perfect hero, which was called Arcadian, was the shepherd-knight. The shepherd represented the peaceful, kind and generous nature, which looks after others, whilst the knight signified the warrior, aggressive and war-like, but only in defence of purity and truth, or of the weak, poor and needy. The shepherd looks after truth, whilst the knight goes in search of truth. The Elizabethan poet, Edmund Spenser, portrayed these two separately in *The Shepheards Calendar* and *The Faerie Queene*, the former being a pastoral poem about the shepherd's life and the latter being a heroic poem about the knights of the Round Table. Sir Philip Sydney combined the two in his *Arcadia*. The whole of *As You Like It* is filled with both these symbols—the shepherds and the knights. The knights are from the court; the shepherds (with the exception of Rosalind and Celia, who become shepherds) are from the forest. The characters who fuse the two together, symbolically, are Rosalind and Orlando, Celia and Oliver, and Touchstone and Audrey.

Friendship & Strife

A further polarity, which was recognised as being of major significance in life by the Orphics, is that of friendship and strife. Friendship was denoted by Venus, and strife by Mars. In fact, the two were portrayed as the twin pillars of the universe, and all Classical temples were distinguished by a portal whose side pillars represented the god and goddess, just as the Egyptians and Persians had their great pylons and Solomon had his brazen pillars. The triumphal arch also has this symbolism.

The Wisdom of Shakespeare in *As You Like It*

The mythological story of the love affair between
Venus (Aphrodite) and Mars (Ares) was devised to
conceal (and reveal) the universal relationship of
friendship and strife in all matters. By striving
together in friendship we can overcome all obstacles
and create harmony, beauty and, ultimately, joy.
Hence, in the myth, Mars and Venus have a child
called Hermione or Harmony, who is represented by
the goddess Ceres (Demeter). She in turn has a child
called Persephone, who represents beauty; and
Persephone has a child named Dionysus, or Bacchus,
who signifies joy or illumination. Dionysus-Bacchus is
the god of Drama, whose particular form of drama was
known as the Mysteries. He was revered as the divine
Poet or Bard.

Shakespeare celebrated part of this great myth and
Mystery quite openly in his *Winter's Tale,* but its principles underlie all his plays, including *As You Like It.*
Occasionally he allows these basic polarities to show
more clearly and symbolically, such as in the scene in
As You Like It (I, ii) where Celia promises everlasting
friendship to her cousin Rosalind. This is immediately
followed, on the same spot, by the wrestling match
between Charles and Orlando. Then, as a result of this
'striving', Rosalind falls in love with Orlando, and he
with her. The wrestling, however, also has another and
entirely different effect, for it is followed immediately
by the anger of Duke Frederick, leading to the banishment of Rosalind and outlawing of Orlando.

In this early scene we have strife and friendship
portrayed dramatically as the key event which precipitates the action of the play. Basically it is good, and it
acts as a gateway to the rest of the story. However,
Shakespeare immediately follows the good manifestation

of these principles by portraying their shadow or negative echo—the warlike actions and enmity of Duke Frederick. In doing this, Shakespeare first shows the 'twin pillars' from the 'light' point of view and then, secondly, from the 'dark' or 'shadow' point of view. Taking each pair as a unit, the two pairs (*i.e.* strife-friendship and war-enmity) also show, as polarities to each other, the twin pillars of the universe; but this time as light and dark, or love and hate, good and evil.

Lost & Found

As part of this same Mystery, *As You Like It* tells the tale of a daughter who is lost and then found again, like Perdita in *The Winter's Tale.* In *As You Like It* the lost daughter is Rosalind. She is forcibly estranged from her father, unlike the story of Perdita, whose father orders her to be cast away; but the result is the same. In each case, and after a time filled with experiences, the daughter is joyfully reunited with her father and marriages take place.

This 'lost and found' theme is that of the great Mystery of Demeter and Persephone that used to be acted out annually in the Mystery schools of Greece and Rome—the most famous of these initiatic training centres being Eleusis (near Athens) in Greece and Cumæ (near Naples) in Italy. In the myth, Persephone is abducted by Hades and taken into the underworld. Eventually she is found by Hermes (Mercury) and, striking a bargain with Hades, is restored to her mother's realm for part of each year. During the rest of the year (the winter part) she has to return to Hades and the underworld, where she is the queen. In this myth is concealed the mystery of life, it being an allegory of the human soul as well as of the vital forces of nature.

4. Initiatory Themes

Sir Oliver de Boys & his Three Sons

All Shakespeare's Comedies are Mysteries, and all Mysteries are dramas of initiation in which heroes and heroines enter fully into the mysterious nature of life. In doing so they transform an existing situation into a far better state of affairs. Moreover, they find true life, which is love, by facing death. They do this by offering their own lives in order to save the lives of others.[20]

In the Orphic Mysteries, the underworld (known as Tartarus) is the place of the living dead, and Persephone faces death in her experience in the underworld. She has to learn to rise above its dangers and terrors, and become Queen of Tartarus. Mercury also has to descend into Tartarus, his task being to find and rescue Persephone, and to bring her back to her mother's celestial world.

By Tartarus, the underworld, the ancient philosophers meant the phenomenal world of nature—the physical universe and physical world. It is into this underworld—the Forest of Arden—that Rosalind, accompanied by Celia, is cast when she is banished from the court, just as her father was banished many years before. Close on their heels follows Orlando, accompanied by good old Adam. These two—Orlando and Rosalind—are the key players in this drama. Their stories are initiation dramas and, besides the main story of the play, their evolutionary path contains three major initiatory themes which are worth looking at. Significantly, Orlando's story is bound up with that of his brothers.

The Three Grades of Human development

Certain fairy tales, such as Cinderella, are allegories of the path of initiation of the human soul. As such, they are like the Classical myths that provide the story-lines for the Mysteries. They also have a historical basis, for the truths which the allegories represent are repeatedly manifesting themselves in human affairs. When, as in the fairy tale of Cinderella or the mythological history of Noah, there are three daughters or three sons in the story, it is usually the youngest who is the hero or heroine. The eldest, by contrast, usually appears as the 'bad guy', and often (but not always) seems to be a rather brutal or over-bearing ruler, sometimes even a cruel tyrant. In other words, there is a gradation from harshness to gentleness, from power to love, from greed to generosity, in the family hierarchy. This is not by accident, and the three brothers of the De Boys family in *As You Like It* show the hidden meaning of this particularly well.

The different ages of the brothers represent different ages or periods in the evolution of the human being. The eldest, therefore, personifies the earliest period of human development, whilst the youngest signifies the latest and therefore the best so far. The threesome is chosen because it encapsulates a law which produces three main stages of human evolution in any cycle.

Plato summed this up when he described the first stage as that of the ignorant man who is in servitude to his

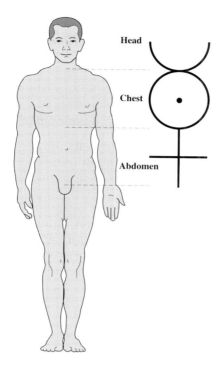

MERCURY–THE BODY AS A TRINITY

animal nature, the second stage as that of the partly informed man who is in servitude to his intellectual nature, and the third stage as that of the divinely enlightened man who is united with the spiritual principle that is the sustaining power in the midst of his being. In other words, the three main developments of the human being are: (1) the sensual and sometimes brutish person, (2) the intellectual person, and (3) the intuitively aware, loving person.

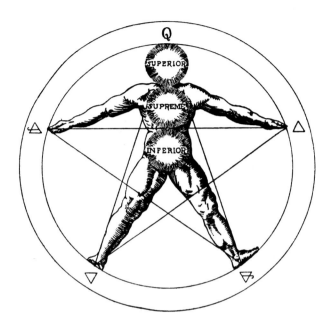

THE PYTHAGOREAN PENTALPHA
from John Reuchlin's *Explication of the Pythagorean Doctrine*
reproduced in Manly P. Hall's *Man, the Grand Symbol of the Mysteries*

These three levels of development are related as foci of will and consciousness to the three main areas of the human body—the abdomen, the head and the chest respectively, with the seat of divinity in the heart. To help us remember this truth, the ancient sages devised the alchemical sign of Mercury to remind us, it being composed of an elemental or equal-armed cross for the abdomen, a crescent moon for the head, and the sun symbol for the chest and heart. The Pythagorean and Neoplatonic philosophers, in a tradition that carried on through the Renaissance, referred to these areas as 'inferior', 'superior' and 'supreme', relating them to the three worlds or divisions of the universe, as may be seen in the accompanying diagram from John Reuchlin's *Explication of the Pythagorean Doctrine.* Modern translations of the Greek myths name these regions of the universe as the underworld, the world and heaven, ruled respectively by Hades and Hestia, Poseidon and Demeter, and Zeus and Hera. These correspond to the physical or natural, the psychological or celestial, and the spiritual or super-celestial realms of the universe. They in turn are associated with the body, soul and spirit of all things.

Plotinus, the 3rd century Neoplatonic philosopher, expressed this truth in terms of knowledge: 'Knowledge has three degrees—Opinion, Science, Illumination. The means or instrument of the first is sense; of the second, dialectic; of the third, intuition.'[21] Greek society was organised to take account of these gradations and differences between people, providing three corresponding levels of education and participation in their society: (1) State religion and ceremonial, (2) Academies, and (3) the Mysteries.

In Shakespeare's *Merchant of Venice,* the three caskets used in the lottery (gold, silver and lead), and the three contenders for Portia's hand in marriage (Morocco, Arragon and Bassanio) who each choose a particular casket suited to their own character, represent the same truth and the same sequence.[22] The prize (Portia's image) is encased in the dull lead, the outer form disguising the precious jewel within, whilst the richly ostentatious gold encases a death's head, and the glamorous silver a fool's head. In *As You Like It*, Touchstone makes it clear that to him his Audrey is like the lead casket: her foulness, like an oyster, contains a pearl. In the fairy tales the youngest brother (or sister) seems, at first, to be the least likely hero, the innate strength and beauty lying hidden behind outer dullness and dirt. The eldest has all the power and wealth, and the next eldest comes a good second in the glamour show of intellect and fashion.

In *As You Like It,* these three stages are clearly defined by the three De Boys brothers:

1. Oliver – Senses/Instinct – Inferior – Will Power

2. Jaques – Reason/Intellect – Superior – Intelligence

3. Orlando – Intuition/Illumination – Supreme – Love-Wisdom

Oliver de Boys is the eldest son and inherits the house and major part of his father's wealth. He is given the power and authority—and responsibility—to look after the upbringing and education of his two younger brothers. However, he acts brutally and abuses his responsibility, controlling the household and Orlando by force, and desiring Orlando's inheritance for himself.

Jaques de Boys, the middle brother, is sent away to school where he flourishes. He is the intellectual. His only spoken role in the play is to report the news at the end, that Duke Frederick is become a converted man.

Orlando de Boys, the youngest brother, is kept beneath his natural station and treated like a servant, with no education or training given him and his inheritance withheld. But he breaks free and proves that he is 'Signior Love', with courage and strength like Hercules. As he goes through his different experiences and overcomes each challenge successfully, so everything else changes with him. Like Hercules, he is both the catalyst and the mercurial solvent.

Orlando and Hercules

The analogy with Hercules is not far fetched. It is actually made in the play by Rosalind, when at the start of the wrestling match she gives Orlando her blessing and prayer: 'Now Hercules be thy speed, young man!' (I, ii, 198). Then what follows has episodes borrowed directly from the myth of Hercules, showing that this is what Shakespeare had in mind.

The Wrestling Match

One of the challenges that Hercules had to meet was a wrestling match with the giant Antaeus. Because Antaeus drew his strength from the earth, he was invincible as long as his feet touched the ground. Hercules overcame the giant by lifting him up and holding him in the air in a vice-like arm grip around his waist until the giant weakened and died.

The remark by Celia, which follows Rosalind's blessing, is related to the way that the giant could lose his strength: 'I would that I were invisible, to catch the strong fellow by the leg' (I, ii, 198). Charles is the strong fellow, the giant. If she (as Celia thought) could only catch Charles' leg and pull it away from under him, so that he should lose firm contact with the ground, then Orlando would have a chance of winning. In the event she doesn't need to do this, as Orlando succeeds on his own and throws Charles. Charles is then described as being unable to speak and has to be carried out. It is possible that he was killed, like Antaeus—maybe in the same manner as Charles himself slew the three young men who challenged him previously.

The Lioness

Hercules, by decree of Zeus (Jupiter), had to be subservient to Eurystheus, king of Argos and Mycenæ. Eurystheus, in an attempt to rid himself of this great hero, set Hercules the most extreme tasks to fulfil, twelve in number. These are known as the Twelve Labours of Hercules, and they have a relationship to the twelve signs and constellations of the Zodiac. When Hercules died, the story relates that the gods took his soul up to heaven and set him in the stars, along with the twelve labours. As a constellation, he has his head touching Ophiuchus, the Æsclepius figure, and his foot on the head of Draco, the Dragon. Such an ascension happened with virtually every other major Greek myth, which themselves are derived from older sources. (The same occurred with the myths of other civilisations the world over.) The stories are in the stars.

The first labour that Hercules had to perform was to kill the lion of Nemea, which was ravaging the country near Mycenæ. This he accomplished by wrestling with the lion and choking it to death with his bare hands.

Orlando also has a lion experience, which he has to slay with his bare hands, only in his case it is a lioness (IV, iii, 113-132). Whilst walking in the forest, he comes upon his brother Oliver sleeping under an old oak. Oliver is threatened by a ravenous lioness, coached ready for the kill in a nearby bush. In order to save his brother, Orlando engages the lioness and slays her.

The Snake

The second labour which Hercules had to undertake was to kill the Lernæan hydra. This was an enormous and highly poisonous snake with multiple heads (some say seven, others nine, or fifty, or a hundred). No sooner had he crushed one head with his club than the hydra grew two more in its place. It would have been impossible to kill had not Hercules had the bright idea of asking his friend Iolas to cauterise with his torch the root of each head as soon as he had crushed it.

Orlando also encounters a snake which, like the lioness, threatens his brother's life (IV, iii, 107-113). This snake—a poisonous one—is wrapped around the neck of his sleeping brother when Orlando arrives on the scene, and is moving its head ever closer to Oliver's mouth, ready to strike. The arrival of Orlando frightens the snake and it slips away into the bush in which the lioness is crouching.

The Stag

The third labour of Hercules was a stag hunt. He had to capture and bring alive into the presence of Eurystheus a stag, famous not only for its remarkable swiftness but also its golden antlers and brazen feet. It took Hercules a whole year to capture the animal, which he finally did by wounding it with an arrow and slowing it down. Having caught it, he threw the animal over his shoulder to carry it home to Eurystheus. The goddess Diana was upset at the hurt given the animal, which was sacred to her, and snatched the stag from Hercules. However, she gave it back to him when he explained to her that he had captured it only in order to fulfil his labour.

Orlando is not actually portrayed as responsible for wounding a stag, although we know that all the lords attending on the elder Duke in the forest, which includes Orlando when he joins them, hunt deer. Celia even describes Orlando as 'furnished like a hunter' after she had secretly discovered him under an oak tree (III, ii, 241), just to make the analogy clear. But the wounded stag episode does occur, early on in the forest scenes, when the lords speak to the Duke concerning Jaques grieving at the hurt of a stag, wounded by a hunter, which came to languish near him (II, i, 21-63). Jaques in this instance is feeling and expressing the grief of the goddess Diana.

Diana is in fact the goddess of the hunt, even though she grieves for any deer that are wounded and in pain. The hunter's victory, when a stag has been successfully hunted and killed well (which is especially difficult when the hunters are on foot), is celebrated in a complete scene of its own (IV, ii). This would seem to stress its importance to the allegory, as well as being a dramatic contrivance to allow a couple of hours to appear to elapse, to suit the story. It is true that hunting scenes were popular with Elizabethan audiences, hunting being perhaps the premier sport for the court, the gentry and the nobility of England; but there is more to this scene than that. A great deal is made of the deer's horns—the antlers of a stag that has just been killed—and of carrying the stag home. The hunter who killed the stag is to wear the antlers as a trophy and 'branch of victory', and he is to be sung home whilst 'the rest shall bear this burden' (*i.e.* the body of the dead stag).

The Four Labours

In terms of the Herculean myth, the wrestling match is not strictly one of the Twelve Labours, but it is nevertheless an important task which Hercules undertakes of his own accord, without being coerced. The challenge with the snake, the lion and the stag are, however, three of the labours—and, moreover, they are the first three.

That Shakespeare should have chosen these is very significant. Orlando's wrestling match with the champion Charles is, as with Hercules, initiated by himself of his own free will: the other three labours are not, which again matches the Herculean story. Not only is the choice of labours significant, but also the order that Shakespeare has selected, for these tell a story in themselves. This is emphasised by them not being in the same order as in the Hercules legend.

1. The wrestling match begins the train of events that make up the story of *As You Like It.* It is the impulse which gets everything going. In addition it is associated with the element earth, for that is where the giant Antaeus gained his strength.

2. The snake is the more esoteric symbol of Scorpio, one of the twelve constellations of the Zodiac. As such, it is associated with the generative organs and powers, which Scorpio is said to rule. It is, of course, also a symbol of the fiery *kundalini* or dragon energy that rises up the spine of the human being and which, when fully arisen to the crown, can bring illumination. But it can be poisonous and deadly if not aroused in love. In the play, the snake is wrapped around the neck of the sleeping Jaques and about to strike at his mouth and tongue. Not only is Scorpio related to the sign of Taurus, which rules the throat, mouth and tongue, but it depicts Oliver as about to receive a throat wound.

3. The lioness, like the lion, is an emblem of the heart. In the sky it is Leo, the Lion, another of the twelve constellations of the Zodiac. Being feminine, the lioness represents the feminine quality of the heart which, at its best, is a gentle, constant strength of love. However, the lioness in *As You Like It* is ravenous and deadly dangerous. She is about to hurt Oliver—to rip out his heart, to which the creature is equated, and devour it.

4. The stag, with its great horns, like Aries the Ram, is representative of the aspirational thoughts and illumination of the head, and is a creature of Diana, the moon goddess. Like the eagle, it is represented in tradition as an enemy of the snake, being its symbolic polarity. Because of the way its antlers are renewed each year, it is also a symbol of death and regeneration. It often appears in emblems with a crucifix between its horns, as in the story of St. Hubert. The wounding of the stag in the hunt is an action which causes hurt. The antlers of the dead creature, however, will grace the head of the hunter.

To summarise, as depicted in the play:

1. The wrestling match begins everything. It is the source of all the rest and is associated with the element earth.

2. the snake is associated with the generative powers seated in the abdomen, but also it is about to deliver a wound to the throat.

3. The lioness is associated with the desires and love of the heart, seated in the chest, but is also about to tear that heart open.

4. The stag is associated with the thoughts and illumination of the head, but is wounded in the haunch and hunted to the death.

In the symbolism of the latter three, each has a double association. The snake, lioness and stag are symbols of the abdomen, the chest and the head respectively, and of will power (or generative power), love and intelligence. The wounds, though, make a sequence known as the Grail Wounds. The Grail King is said to be wounded in three places when there is a lack of virtue in his people, and the Grail land lies waste as a result. The three wounds are to the throat, heart and groin, and they signify a lack of love, lack of understanding and a lack of good action or service respectively and in that order: for desire leads to thought which leads to action.[23] All three issue from an initial impulse which sets things going. To heal the Grail King and the land of the Grail, the wounds have to be healed in the right order, which is the same sequence as in the natural process of life: first we learn to love, then to understand, then to serve. In serving we die well (psychologically), as living sacrifices, and are resurrected or reborn into a higher cycle of consciousness, manifestation and experience.

In the story of *As You Like It*, Orlando plays the part of the Grail Knight who heals the wounds of the Grail King, and in doing so discovers and is given charge of the Holy Grail. This Holy Grail is a vessel of light and life. It is a state of knowledge and joy, but it is also symbolised by the virgin—a woman who is pure in love, understanding and service—whom the Grail Knight can marry and thereafter protect, as her guardian. In the play, Rosalind is this pure person, the one who is married by Orlando.

5. Cycles of Initiation

Initiation

Initiation is based on the natural process of life that each human being is involved with all the time, which can be described as 'impulse-desire-thought-action', repeated over and over again. For each of us, some kind of impulse—spiritual, psychological or physical, either external or internal—produces a desire. The desire leads to a thought about that desire and how we might fulfil it, thereby producing a decision which culminates in an action. When the action is complete, a new impulse begins a fresh sequence, often arising as a direct result of the preceding sequence unless something else interrupts it.

For these reasons the process of life can be perceived as a cycle, each cycle taking place within a time period, large or small, and with smaller cycles operating within larger ones. That is to say, we might wake up one morning and desire to go to work, but as we carry out that desire, with all the thinking and activity it requires, we will also be involved in lots of smaller desires, thoughts and actions, such as getting washed and dressed, going to the toilet, having breakfast, and so on.

This process of life becomes initiation when we consciously and deliberately try to make our process into a far better expression of life, for good. That is to say, when we change our desires into purely loving ones, our thoughts into a deep understanding, and our actions into service that is beneficial to ourselves, others and all forms life. The key to this lies in our desire, which is the motivating force behind what we do. The ultimate start of initiation is to desire only one thing—love: to be loving, to think loving thoughts, to express love in action. This is initiation, which means 'an entering into' the Mystery of divine Love.

The Mystery itself is a 'play'—an acting out or expressing of love in this world, in a myriad of different ways. As Shakespeare perceptively points out, speaking through the mouth of Jaques, all the world's a stage and we are the actors on it (II, vii, 139-140):

> *Jaques.* All the world's a stage,
>   And all the men and women merely players.

Jaques continues, in his characteristic melancholic vein, to enumerate the seven great acts of this human play (II, vii, 141-166):

> They have their exits and their entrances,
> And one man in his time plays many parts,
> His acts being seven ages. At first the infant,
> Mewling and puking in the nurse's arms.
> Then, the whining school-boy with his satchel
> And shining morning face, creeping like a snail
> Unwillingly to school. And then the lover,
> Sighing like a furnace, with a woeful ballad
> Made to his mistress' eyebrow. Then, a soldier,
> Full of strange oaths, and bearded like the pard,
> Jealous in honour, sudden, and quick in quarrel,
> Seeking the bubble reputation

Cycles of Initiation

> Even in the cannon's mouth. And then, the justice,
> In fair round belly, with good capon lin'd,
> With eyes severe, and beard of formal cut,
> Full of wise saws, and modern instances,
> And so he plays his part. The sixth age shifts
> Into the lean and slipper'd pantaloon,
> With spectacles on nose, and pouch on side,
> His youthful hose well sav'd, a world too wide
> For his shrunk shank, and his big manly voice,
> Turning again toward childish treble, pipes
> And whistles in his sound. Last scene of all,
> That ends this strange eventful history,
> Is second childishness and mere oblivion,
> Sans teeth, sans eyes, sans taste, sans everything.

This is a perceptive but thoroughly pessimistic analysis of human life, the morbidness of which is immediately contradicted by the entrance of Orlando with Adam, who both belie Jaques' description of their respective ages. However, Jaques is right in one thing, our lives do have a pattern of seven ages to them, each of distinct character, and this is related to the cycle of life and initiation just described.

Desire, thought and action proceed from some impulse, the origin of the other three. Hence it is said that a trinity issues from a unity, expressing that unity: just as the three aspects of spiritual light (*i.e.* love, wisdom and power) are born from the primordial darkness and express that divine darkness. When the action is complete, if we pause and learn from it, we can begin a fresh cycle with the advantage of knowledge and do things better than before. If we follow the path of initiation, then our loving, understanding and service will produce knowledge of truth, which is a joy, an illumination. We will know we have done well, we will enjoy having been useful and having given joy to others as a result, and we will have discovered something that is true.

The ancient philosophers saw an analogy in this process with the candle, which begins in its unlighted state as hard, cold, 'dead' wax; but which, when lit with a match of some kind, produces its own light. To do this, the hard wax melts into a liquid, the liquid vaporises, and the vapour bursts into flame. In the flame is light, which the flame gives birth to as its 'child'. Thus the candle transforms from an original 'earthy' state into a 'watery' state, then an 'airy' state, and finally a 'fiery' state. From the flame shines the quintessence, light, which is useful, illuminating and joyful.

If we continue in a second cycle of life which makes use of the joy and enlightenment produced in the first cycle, we can perform wonders. In such a second cycle, with joy as our starting impulse, the loving emotion is enriched into a strong, creative love; the understanding is transformed into a wisdom; and the service into a truly noble and powerful act of good that can produce miracles. In the candle analogy this is represented by the four aspects of the shining light— the 'sun' in the flame, the radiance, the reflection and the heat.

When the two cycles are totted up, there are a total of seven stages derived from the initial lighting of the candle. For this reason the ancients described seven stages or degrees of initiation in their Mystery schools, the first three degrees belonging to the Lesser Mysteries and the last four comprising the Greater Mysteries of Initiation. In this, there is also a corre-spondence with the musical octave and with the seven colours of prismatic light. In other words, it exhibits a universal law.

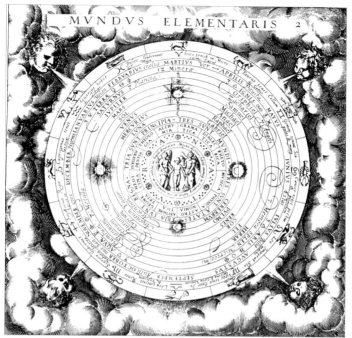

ALCHEMICAL MANDALA FROM "THE ALL WISE DOORKEEPER"
contained in the *Musaeum Hermeticum* of 1625
reproduced by kind permission from:
The Western Mandala Hermetic Research Series No.3

So, although Jaques is not recounting the stages of initiation in his description of a man's life, he is making a pointed reference to the same law which produces seven recognisable stages of growth and decay in each human life span, which begin from the impulse of birth. He describes what might be called the mundane life cycle of a person who is not treading the path of initiation. Orlando and Jaques, by contrast, are treading the initiatory path to light and happiness.

The four alchemical elements (earth, water, air and fire) are used in the Hermetic tradition to symbolise the four stages of one complete cycle (*e.g.* impulse-desire-thought-action), just as they are manifested physically in the phenomenon of the burning candle.

A double cycle is further represented symbolically by the Earth plus the seven sacred planets—Moon, Mercury, Venus, Mars, Jupiter, Saturn and Sun—only Jaques' Sun is, sadly, 'mere oblivion'. The infant comes under the mothering influence of the Moon, the school-boy under Mercury, the lover under Venus. Then, from the stage of lover there is a transformation into the soldier under the influence of Mars, followed by the justice under Jupiter and the pantaloon under Saturn. The last scene of all, if we have made the effort to live a good life, is the happy, illuminated state of bliss represented by the Sun, in which our soul, shining now like a sun, will arise from our physical body and join the greater Sun, the Soul of the universe.

This progression through the ages of a human life span parallels the ancient concept of the soul's ascent through the heavens, which are likewise represented by the seven sacred planets. Only, in regular representations of this scheme, the Sun is normally placed fourth, after Venus, rather than last. If you think about this, to place the Sun, giver of light and life to all the planets, as merely fourth in the hierarchical ladder is strange. Shakespeare would appear to be following a more esoteric and accurate scheme, with deeper meaning.

The ascent through the seven heavens, symbolised by Jacob's Ladder in Hebraic and Christian terminology, is likewise represented in Freemasonry by the seven-runged ladder—the ladder which stands on the earth that supports it. This symbolism is straight out of the ancient

Mystery schools, wherein the ladder was also used to describe the seven stages of initiation which arise from the initial 'earthy' or uninitiated state of being.[24]

The Four Major Life Cycles

Traditionally, four major life cycle patterns are recognised as existing in the human state of evolution. These are levels of human evolution, and comprise the gross, the mundane, the virtuous and the exalted states of existence. Like each individual cycle of life already described, these four are seen to constitute a complete evolutionary cycle and are therefore also symbolised by the four alchemical elements—earth, water, air and fire respectively. The mundane is the ordinary person's life cycle, before his or her 'awakening'. The gross is the perverted life cycle. Only the virtuous and exalted cycles belong to initiation, the former corresponding to the Lesser Mysteries and the latter to the Greater Mysteries of Initiation.

Like many of the other Shakespeare plays, *As You Like It* shows all four cycles in operation in the lives of its characters, *viz.*:

- **Exalted**   Rosalind, Celia, Duke Senior
- **Virtuous**   Orlando, Adam, Touchstone
- **Mundane**   Jaques, Phebe, Audrey, Silvius, Corin
- **Gross**   Duke Frederick, Oliver

Rosalind and Celia display from the start the qualities of initiates who have already been through the virtuous cycle of development. That is to say, they are reasonably 'virgin' or pure in desire, thought and action, and therefore inwardly beautiful. Rosalind's actions throughout the play, including her instruction of Orlando and her culminating act of magic, show her to be following the path of the adept, like Portia in *The Merchant of Venice*, Miranda in *Pericles,* and Prospero in *The Tempest*. Celia, who gives up all for love of her dear friend and helps make the exile bearable and bear fruit, is Rosalind's feminine counterpart or 'twin', as in the relationship of Nerissa to Portia in *The Merchant of Venice.*

The two brothers whom these two princesses marry at the end of the play help to emphasise the 'twinship' of Rosalind and Celia. Orlando and Oliver, however, do not begin at the same level of initiation as the ladies—a circumstance which is further emphasised symbolically by the difference in social standing between the two princesses and the two men, who may be gentlemen, sons of a knight, but who certainly are not lords or princes. The fact that Shakespeare keeps the title of the two women as princesses, as in his source story, whilst changing the two kings to dukes to suit his Ardennes setting, shows the importance he attached to this hierarchical difference in respect of the two women. They are exalted: the others (with the exception of the elder Duke) are not—although they may, with effort, become so.

Oliver begins in the corrupt cycle, with his hate and maltreatment of his younger brother, his material greed and evil intents, and his misuse and abuse of his responsible and privileged status. Orlando, by contrast, has from the start a good heart but little education. His path becomes the hero's path, which takes him through the lesser mysteries of initiation, the virtuous cycle, with Rosalind as the personal love and ideal which drives him on. In this, Orlando 'saves' or redeems Oliver by his personal act of bravery and charity. He lifts his brother out of a gross cycle of behaviour and into a mundane cycle, in which Oliver is able to meet and fall in love with Celia, and she with him. Her love for him then lifts Oliver into a virtuous cycle of initiation, in which he surrenders his worldly wealth for more heavenly things. In a similar way Rosalind, through her love and self-sacrifice for Orlando, lifts Orlando towards a higher level, until, when they marry, he achieves and enters her exalted realm of life. Together with Orlando on the hero's path is Touchstone and Adam, each following it in their own ways, sacrificing all in charity for those they love and serve.

The linking of Orlando and Oliver with Rosalind and Celia, through love, courtship and marriage, is a direct representation of the link that exists between the virtuous and the exalted cycles of initiation, which the seven-runged ladder expresses. Moreover, just as a heavenly ladder of initiation exists for the twinned virtuous and exalted cycles, so an earthly ladder of evolution exists for the inter-linked gross and mundane cycles. The main point of it all, which is the purpose of life, is for each character to climb the ladders of earthly and heavenly evolution and initiation, helped by each other and especially by those above.

A further point worth noting is that, once we have climbed one ladder of initiation, we will discover that life is so vastly abundant and unlimited that there are further ladders to mount. One ladder can turn out to be but the first rung of a second, greater ladder. Adeptship at one level may be but discipleship at another. Hence it is of immense significance that Rosalind states, as Ganymede, that she has been taught by a great magician. It may indeed be a kind of fantasy foisted on the others in Rosalind's purpose of creating psychological magic, but she is no liar. The magician does indeed exist; for

Rosalind, like everyone else, is taught by another greater than her—the greatest of all being the still, small voice of love in the heart, which speaks wisdom and truth to our minds.

Other than the divine voice or Word of God within her heart, Rosalind is also referring subtly to her father who, like the magus Prospero, is the 'great magician, obscured in the circle of this forest', who is 'most profound in his art and yet not damnable', and with whom she has conversed since she was three years old (v, ii, 60-63; v, iv, 30-34). This magician is a very definite person. She tells the others that he is her uncle, but it is certainly not Duke Frederick. The 'magician' can only be her father, the true Duke (*i.e.* the 'old Duke' or 'Duke Senior'), who is proclaimed to be a good man.

As You Like It is a play, but it is also a perceptive commentary on real life. Like life, it can be seen as a game as well as a play, in each of which we are players, and which the game of Snakes and Ladders was devised to portray. In Shakespeare's Comedies, all the main characters successfully climb their ladders, which is the nature of such comedy; whereas in the Histories and Tragedies many succumb to the snakes, the alternative and treacherous aspect of life.

'As You Like It' Cycle of Initiation

Jaques' commentary on the seven ages of man do, in fact, sound the key-note that describes the initiatic structure of the whole play. The group of eight persons who fall in love and join in marriage also sounds the same note, reinforced by Hymen when he says, 'Here's eight that must take hands to join in Hymen's bands, if truth holds true contents' (v, iv, 127-130).

Cycles of Initiation

Taking the cue from Jaques and analysing the play from the point of view of these cycles of life and initiation, it can be discovered that *As You Like It* has eight main sections (or seven that arise from the initial beginning), and each section is composed of four main parts. That is to say, each section is a complete cycle in itself. As is fairly usual, the five acts and twenty-two scenes, which the play is divided into for the purposes of dramatisation, do not bear much relationship to this more hidden structure; but the structure exists nonetheless, like the carefully devised rhythm and beat of the poetry. Hidden structures such as these undoubtedly constitute one of those factors which make the Shakespeare plays great. It is alchemical magic in the true Hermetic and Magian tradition.

The eight sections of the play follow the pattern of the sacred planets, described above, beginning with the 'Earth' and culminating with the 'Sun'. Within this eight-fold framework, examples of the four major cycles (gross, mundane, virtuous and exalted) are portrayed running concurrently, each being undergone by different characters who interact with and help each other. These major evolutionary and initiatory cycles are not sequential in the sense of showing any single person traversing first a lower major cycle and then a higher major cycle, except in the one instance of Oliver, who is raised from a gross cycle to a mundane and then a virtuous cycle during the course of the play. All other transmutations from one major cycle to the next higher are accomplished at the end of the play.

What the structure of the play does do, however, is provide a sequence of eight minor cycles which the characters of the play experience as a group, each minor cycle portraying the 'impulse-desire-thought-action' structure and process of life. These eight minor cycles form a 'ladder', which itself constitutes one major double-cycle in which a whole society is transformed for the better in a dramatic life-changing way.

In terms of this major double-cycle, its first cycle (comprising the first four minor cycles) begins with the situation of Rosalind separated from her father and ends with the attempted unworthy wedding of Touchstone and Audrey. The second cycle (comprising the second set of four minor cycles), by contrast, begins with Rosalind meeting her father and joining with him again, howbeit in disguise, and ends with a truly worthy wedding, not only of Touchstone and Audrey but also of Rosalind and Orlando, Oliver and Celia, and Silvius and Phebe. The earlier attempted marriage would have been surreptitious, hasty and meanly witnessed, whilst the actual concluding marriage takes place in a real circle of love, composed of all strata of society, and is witnessed and blessed by the good Duke and all his noble followers, and by Hymen, god of marriage.

The group aspect is complex but is an important factor of life, for, as the saying goes, no one is an island. We help or hinder each other. Moreover, by raising ourselves higher on the ladder, we automatically generate the conditions to assist or enable others to rise, even if we do not seem to be directly involved with those other persons. Shakespeare shows both the direct and indirect influences dramatically in the play, wherein, for instance, Orlando is seen to directly help his brother Oliver, whilst the conversion of Duke Frederic is a seemingly remote event but nevertheless the result of what the others have accomplished and changed in themselves.

Cycles of Initiation

The majority of people in our human society tend to find such remote effects of our individual and group behaviour a hard truth to grasp or even think about. Therefore it happens that many audiences find the sudden conversion of Duke Frederick in *As You Like It* to be a contrived fantasy of Shakespeare's, suitable only for his type of fairy-tale comedy. However, it is all far more true to life than many realise and has often been taught by the great teachers of humanity. The truth is well expressed in the modern (but misnamed) Chaos theory with its proposition of the 'butterfly effect', which suggests that a butterfly stirring its wings in Beijing can later affect the weather of New York.

In *As You Like It*, whilst Orlando, helped by Adam, faces the dangers of the forest, performs his acts of charity and is taught by 'Ganymede', so Rosalind, assisted by Celia, develops her adeptship, working creatively with love, wisdom and, finally, magical power. As a result of all this, first Orlando's brother Oliver and then Duke Frederick are raised out of their gross levels of behaviour, suddenly, into much higher and potentially virtuous cycles. In the background, the deposed Duke, a good man who works through an adept's cycle of testing and training in the forest, is restored to his rightful position in the world but at a much higher level of initiation. Touchstone finds comfort in the honest Audrey; and Jaques, finding that his mood does not fit with those who live life with love and zest, moves on to new subjects for his melancholic study of human nature.

An analysis of the play is given in the accompanying tables:

1. Table 1 presents the eight sections (or minor cycles) of the play, each with its four parts.

2. Table 2 presents Orlando's story, which is comprised of three successive personal cycles, all at the virtuous level.

3. Table 3 presents Rosalind's story, which is comprised of four successive personal cycles at the exalted level.

4. Table 4 presents Oliver's story, which covers three personal cycles: the first at the gross level, the second at the mundane level, and the third at the virtuous level.

5. Table 5 outlines Duke Senior's story, consisting of one personal cycle at the exalted level of initiation.

6. Table 6 outlines Duke Frederick's story, comprising one personal cycle at the gross level of human behaviour.

There are certain features which help identify each section or minor cycle. For instance, the first stage of a cycle contains the material or event that either provides the impulse for the unfolding of the following stages or at least sets the scene in some way. The second stage expresses mainly desires or emotions, which are also associated with song (*i.e.* music of the heart) and movement (*i.e.* e-motion). The third stage is focused primarily on thinking—on ideas, discussions, advice, explanations, plans, announcements, looking and seeing. The fourth stage, which completes each cycle, deals with the action or final outcome of that cycle, which, in initiation, involves an act of charity or self-sacrifice, sometimes represented as a shedding of blood. Being the final stage, it is associated with death or the threat of death—certainly a psychological death—and also with feasting and marriage; although, in the final section of the play, marriage and the marriage feast is the main theme of the whole section, being the culmination of the play. The final stage can also involve a rapid change of circumstances, such as the fleeing of the princesses at the end of the first minor cycle and of Orlando and Adam at the end of the second minor cycle, and the enforced sending of Oliver to the forest to find his brother at the end of the third minor cycle.

The tables use the symbolism of the four alchemical elements (earth, water, air, fire) to identify the four stages of each cycle. In addition, in Table 1 the symbolism of the planets (Earth, Moon, Mercury, Venus, Mars, Jupiter, Saturn, Sun) are used to identify each of the eight successive minor cycles in the story of the play, so that Shakespeare's organisation of the play can be more easily seen.

Table 1 – The Eight Cycles of As You Like It

Cycle (Section)	Stage (Element)	Act, Scene	As You Like It story
1 EARTH	EARTH	I, i	(Prologue) Orlando, with Adam in the Orchard, complains about Oliver's treatment of him and that he can stand it no longer.
		I, i	Orlando fights with Oliver and makes his brother promise to give him his proper due.
		I, i	Charles gives the news at court, that the old Duke is banished.
		I, i	Oliver sets up Orlando to be killed by Charles in the wrestling match.
	WATER	I, ii	Celia tries to cheer up Rosalind, who is depressed about her father's banishment, and declares her undying love for her friend.
		I, ii	Orlando wrestles with Charles and wins.
		I, ii	Duke Frederick is incensed against Orlando, refusing to give him the prize.
		I, ii	Rosalind gives Orlando her chain: they fall in love with each other.
	AIR	I, ii	Orlando advised to flee Duke Frederick's wrath.
	FIRE	I, iii	Duke Frederick banishes Rosalind.
		I, iii	Celia volunteers to leave her father and go with her friend into exile, to seek Rosalind's father, the true Duke, in the Forest of Arden. They disguise themselves for their journey and go to fetch Touchstone for company.

2 MOON	EARTH	II, i	The banished Duke and his company discuss life in the forest. Jaques' lament for a wounded deer is reported to the Duke.
	WATER	II, i	The Duke desires immediately to join Jaques, to learn more matter.
	AIR	II, ii II, iii	Duke Frederick tries to find Rosalind and Celia. He orders the arrest of Oliver, planning to use him to find the princesses. Adam warns Orlando that Oliver means to kill him.
	FIRE	II, iii	Adam persuades Orlando to flee, offering all his saved money and himself in Orlando's service. Orlando accepts and they flee together.
3 MERCURY	EARTH	II, iv	Rosalind and Celia, both disguised, together with Touchstone, arrive in the Forest of Arden. They meet Corin and Silvius, shepherds. Corin tells them that the cottage and sheep are for sale. The princesses decide to buy them and ask Corin to arrange the purchase.
	WATER	II, v II, v	Amiens, Jaques and other lords prepare a picnic in the forest. Amiens and Jaques sing about the austere forest life.
	AIR	II, vi II, vii.	Orlando and Adam arrive in Arden. Adam collapses. Orlando decides to carry Adam till they find shelter and food. The Duke and his followers are about to eat their picnic when Jaques joins them late, excited at having met a fool in the forest and explaining how he would like to be a fool.

MERCURY (contd)	FIRE	II, vii. II, vii. III, i	Orlando rushes upon them, demanding food at sword-point. He is courteously invited to join the feast. Whilst Orlando leaves to fetch Adam, the Duke and Jaques make observations about their state and that of the world and mankind. Duke Frederick orders Oliver to find Orlando and bring him back, dead or alive.
4 VENUS	EARTH	III, ii	Orlando wanders through the forest, hanging love poems to Rosalind on the trees.
	WATER	III, ii	Corin and Touchstone walk together and meet Ganymede (Rosalind) reading the poems. The fool ridicules the poetry. Rosalind is angry with him for meddling in her affairs of the heart. Celia joins them, reading another poem.
	AIR	III, ii III, ii	Celia reveals to Rosalind that she has discovered Orlando in the forest. The princesses eavesdrop on Orlando and Jaques arguing about the love poetry. Jaques leaves and Rosalind, as Ganymede, approaches Orlando. She offers to cure him of his love-sickness and he agrees.
	FIRE	III, iii	Touchstone is about to marry Audrey in the forest. Jaques offers to give the bride away, but then persuades Touchstone to arrange a better way to be married.
5 MARS	EARTH	III, iv	Rosalind is upset that Orlando is late for his rendezvous with her. She reveals to Celia that she has met her father in the forest, although he does not recognise her in her disguise. Corin invites them to witness the courtship of Phebe by Silvius.

MARS (contd)	WATER	III, v	Rosalind, Celia and Corin eavesdrop on the wooing. Rosalind, disguised as Ganymede and angry with Phebe at her treatment of Silvius, castigates the shepherdess. Phebe falls in love with Ganymede.
	AIR	IV, i	Jaques and Ganymede discuss melancholy. She derides him for selling his lands.
	FIRE	IV, i IV, i	Orlando arrives late, and she (as Ganymede) berates him for his tardiness. They begin the love-cure and, with Celia's help, undergo a mock marriage. After his departure, Celia castigates Rosalind for misusing the female sex. Rosalind explains how much she is in love with him.
6 JUPITER	EARTH	IV, ii	Jaques and the lords, having hunted and killed a deer, celebrate the feat with song.
	WATER	IV, iii	Rosalind, reading aloud the love poem from Phebe delivered to her by Silvius, reveals to Silvius how false Phebe is to him.
	AIR	IV, iii	Oliver arrives, recognises Ganymede and Aliena by their description, and reportshow Orlando saved his life, revealing who he is and how he is changed because of the incident.
	FIRE	IV, iii	Oliver gives Rosalind the bloody napkin. She swoons at the sight of Orlando's blood.

7 SATURN			
	EARTH	V, i V, ii	Touchstone sees off William, another suitor for Audrey's hand in marriage. Oliver reveals to Orlando how he and Aliena (Celia) have fallen in love and agreed to marry.
	WATER	V, ii	Expressing his newly found love for and friendship with his brother, Oliver promises to surrender to Orlando their family house and revenue, whilst he stays in the forest with Celia.
		V, ii	Oliver asks Orlando for his consent, to which Orlando agrees, promising that the wedding should be celebrated on the morrow, to which he will invite the Duke and all his followers.
	AIR	V, ii	Meeting Ganymede, Orlando makes it clear that he cannot continue with the love-cure, but longs for Rosalind, having seen the happiness in his brother's eyes.
	FIRE	V, ii	Ganymede, claiming to be tutored by a great magician, declares that she can work magic and ensure that when Orlando's brother marries Aliena he will marry Rosalind. She promises to Orlando, Oliver and Phebe that they will be married on the morrow. They, in turn, enthralled by her magic, all promise not to fail.
		V, iii	Touchstone tells Audrey that they are to be married on the morrow. Two pages sing a song for them.

8 SUN	EARTH	V, iv V, iv V, iv V, iv	The Duke and his attendant lords all assemble for the magic and the marriages. Hymen, god of marriage, is conjured up by Ganymede. Rosalind and Celia appear as their true selves. The Duke and his daughter are reunited.
	WATER	V, iv	The four couples—Rosalind and Orlando, Celia and Oliver, Touchstone and Audrey, Phebe and Silvius—are married with the blessing of Hymen and the Duke, as a wedlock hymn is sung.
	AIR	V, iv	Jaques de Boys arrives and announces that Duke Frederick has been converted to a religious life, and that he surrenders the dukedom to his elder brother and restores all confiscated lands and property to the exiled lords.
	FIRE	V, iv	The Duke calls on all to complete the marriage celebrations, after which he will share his fortune with all, according to their measure, and return to court to rule. Jacques decides to join Duke Frederick.
		V, iv	(Epilogue) The play concludes with dancing and Rosalind's Epilogue.

Table 2 — The Story of Orlando

Stage (Element)	Act, Scene	Orlando's story
EARTH	I, i	(Prologue) Orlando, with Adam in the Orchard, complains about Oliver's treatment of him and that he can stand it no longer.
WATER	I, i I, i	Orlando fights with Oliver and makes his brother promise to give him his proper due. Oliver sets up Orlando to be killed by Charles in the wrestling match.
	I, ii	Orlando wrestles with Charles and wins.
	I, ii	Duke Frederick is incensed against Orlando, refusing to give him the prize.
	I, ii	Rosalind gives Orlando her chain: they fall in love with each other.
AIR	I, ii II, iii	Orlando advised to flee Duke Frederick's wrath. Adam warns Orlando that Oliver means to kill him.
	II, iii	Adam persuades Orlando to flee, offering all his saved money and himself in Orlando's service. Orlando accepts and they flee together.

FIRE	II, vi	Orlando and Adam arrive in Arden. Adam collapses. Orlando decides to carry Adam till they find shelter and food.
	II, vii	Orlando discovers the Duke and his followers at their picnic. Believing them to be foresters or outlaws, he rushes upon them, demanding food at sword-point. He is courteously invited to join the feast, but goes to fetch Adam first.
EARTH	★	Orlando joins the Duke and his followers, living and hunting in the forest.
WATER	III, ii	Orlando wanders through the forest, hanging love poems to Rosalind on the trees.
AIR	III, ii	Orlando and Jaques argue about the love poetry. Jaques leaves and Rosalind, as Ganymede, approaches Orlando. She offers to cure him of his love-sickness and he agrees.
	IV, i	Orlando arrives late for his rendezvous, and is berated by Ganymede for his tardiness. They begin the love-cure and, with Celia's help, undergo a mock marriage.
FIRE	★	Whilst walking in the forest Orlando comes upon his brother fast asleep under an oak. Oliver's life is endangered by a snake and a lioness. Orlando frightens away the snake and fights and kills the lioness. Oliver awakes in time to see this happen. Owing his life to his brother, he becomes reconciled with Orlando and a changed man. Orlando leads Oliver to the Duke, who gives him fresh clothes and food.
	★	Orlando is wounded as a result of the fight with the lioness, and made late for his rendezvous with Ganymede. He gives Oliver a napkin stained with his blood and asks his brother to find Ganymede and explain with the help of the napkin why he is late, whilst he recovers from the wound.

EARTH	V, ii	Oliver, having met Ganymede and Aliena, reveals to Orlando how he and Aliena (Celia) have fallen in love and agreed to marry.
WATER	V, ii	Expressing his newly found love for and friendship with his brother, Oliver promises to surrender to Orlando their family house and revenue, whilst he stays in the forest with Celia.
	V, ii	Oliver asks Orlando for his consent, to which Orlando agrees, promising that the wedding should be celebrated on the morrow, to which he will invite the Duke and all his followers.
AIR	V, ii	Meeting Ganymede, Orlando makes it clear that he cannot continue with the love-cure, but longs for Rosalind, having seen the happiness in his brother's eyes.
	V, ii	Ganymede, claiming to be tutored by a great magician, declares that she can work magic and ensure that when Oliver marries Aliena he will marry Rosalind. She promises he will be married on the morrow. He, desperate and persuaded by her magic, promises not to fail.
FIRE	V, iv	Orlando assembles with the Duke and his attendant lords for the magic and the wedding to his beloved Rosalind.
	V, iv	Hymen, god of marriage, is conjured up. Rosalind and Celia appear as their true selves. Orlando marries Rosalind with the blessing of Hymen and the Duke.

Table 3 — The Story of Rosalind

Stage (Element)	Act, Scene	Rosalind's story
EARTH	★	Rosalind's father, the rightful Duke, has been usurped and banished by his younger brother. Rosalind has been kept at court by her uncle, separated from her father.
	I, ii	Celia tries to cheer up Rosalind, who is depressed about her father's banishment, and declares her undying love for her friend.
WATER	I, ii	Rosalind watches Orlando win the wrestling match. She falls in love with him and gives Orlando her chain.
	I, iii	Duke Frederick banishes Rosalind.
AIR	I, iii	Celia volunteers to leave her father and go with her friend into exile, to seek Rosalind's father, the true Duke, in the Forest of Arden. They plan their journey.
FIRE	I, iii	They disguise themselves for their journey and go to fetch Touchstone for company.
EARTH	II, iv II, iv	Rosalind and Celia, both disguised, together with Touchstone, arrive in the Forest of Arden. They meet Corin and Silvius, shepherds. Corin tells them that the cottage and sheep are for sale. The princesses wish to buy them and ask Corin to arrange the purchase.

WATER	III, ii	Rosalind reads Orlando's love poems. Corin and Touchstone meet her, and Touchstone teases her about the poems. She responds angrily at his meddling. Celia joins them, reading another poem.
AIR	III, ii III, ii	Celia reveals to Rosalind that she has discovered Orlando in the forest. The princesses eavesdrop on Orlando and Jaques arguing about the love poetry.
FIRE	III, ii	Rosalind, as Ganymede, approaches Orlando. She offers to cure him of his love-sickness and he agrees.
EARTH	III, iv	Rosalind is upset that Orlando is late for his rendezvous with her. She reveals to Celia that she has met her father in the forest, although he does not recognise her in her disguise. Corin invites them to witness the courtship of Phebe by Silvius.
WATER	III, v	Rosalind, Celia and Corin eavesdrop on the wooing of Phebe by Silvius. Rosalind, disguised as Ganymede and angry with Phebe at her treatment of Silvius, castigates the shepherdess.
AIR	IV, i IV, i	Jaques and Rosalind (as Ganymede) discuss melancholy. She derides him for selling his lands. Orlando arrives late, and she (as Ganymede) berates him for his tardiness.
FIRE	IV, i	They begin the love-cure and, with Celia's help, undergo a mock marriage.

EARTH	IV, i	After his departure, Celia castigates Rosalind for misusing the female sex.
WATER	IV, i	Rosalind explains how much she is in love with him.
AIR	IV, iii	Rosalind, reading aloud the letter from Phebe delivered to her by Silvius, reveals to Silvius how false Phebe is to him.
	IV, iii	Oliver arrives and reports how Orlando saved his life, revealing who he is and how he is changed because of the incident. Rosalind faints at the sight of Orlando's blood on the napkin sent to her.
	V, ii	Orlando makes it clear to Ganymede (Rosalind) that he cannot continue with the love-cure, but longs for Rosalind, having seen the happiness in his brother's eyes.
	V, ii	Rosalind (as Ganymede), claiming to be tutored by a great magician, declares that she can work magic and ensure that when Orlando's brother marries Aliena he will marry Rosalind. She promises to Orlando, Oliver and Phebe that they will be married on the morrow. They, in turn, enthralled by her magic, all promise not to fail.
FIRE	V, iv	The Duke and his attendant lords all assemble before Ganymede (Rosalind) and Aliena (Celia) for the magic and the marriages.
	V, iv	Ganymede (Rosalind) conjures up Hymen, god of marriage. She and Celia then appear as their true selves. She is reunited to her father. Rosalind is married to Oliver, together with the other three couples—Celia and Oliver, Touchstone and Audrey, Phebe and Silvius, with the blessing of Hymen and the Duke.

Table 4 — The Story of Oliver

Stage (Element)	Act, Scene	Oliver's story
EARTH	I, i	Oliver is attacked by and fights with Orlando, but is overcome.
WATER	I, i	Oliver agrees to Orlando's demands for the release of Orlando's inheritance in order to be released from Orlando's grip, but has no intention of fulfilling the demand, desiring the money for himself.
AIR	I, ii	Oliver plans to be rid of Orlando and persuades Charles to try to kill him in the wrestling match.
	II, iii	Hearing that Orlando defeated Charles and is therefore still alive, Oliver plots to kill Orlando in another way.
FIRE	II, vi ★	Oliver is arrested and ordered by Duke Frederick to find Orlando and bring him back, dead or alive. If he fails he will be banished and his estate forfeit. Oliver searches in the Forest of Arden for his brother. Being tired, he lies under a tree to sleep. Whilst asleep, his life is endangered by a snake and a lioness. Orlando discovers his brother sleeping and in danger, frightens away the snake and fights and kills the lioness. Oliver awakes in time to see this happen. Thanking his brother, owing him his life, he becomes reconciled with Orlando and a changed man. He is led by Orlando to the Duke, who gives him fresh clothes and food.

EARTH	IV, iii	Charged by his brother to take a message and a napkin stained with Orlando's blood to Ganymede, Oliver sets out to find 'him' and Aliena at the shepherd's cottage. Discovering them, he reports how Orlando saved his life, revealing who he is and how he is changed because of the incident.
WATER	★	Oliver falls in love with Aliena (Celia) at first sight, and she with him.
AIR	★	Oliver and Aliena discuss marriage and making a life for themselves as shepherds, living at the shepherd's cottage in the forest.
FIRE	★	Oliver and Aliena plight their troth.
EARTH	V, ii	Oliver reveals to Orlando how he and Aliena (Celia) have fallen in love and agreed to marry.
WATER	V, ii	Expressing his newly found love for and friendship with his brother, Oliver promises to surrender to Orlando their family house and revenue, whilst he stays in the forest with Celia.
AIR	V, ii	Oliver asks Orlando for his consent, to which Orlando agrees, promising that the wedding should be celebrated on the morrow, to which he will invite the Duke and all his followers.
FIRE	V, iv	Oliver assembles with the Duke and his attendant lords, and his hopeful brother, for his wedding to Aliena.
	V, iv	Hymen, god of marriage, is conjured up. Rosalind and Celia appear as their true selves. Oliver, knowing now who his love really is, marries Celia in a joint wedding with his brother and Rosalind and the other two couples assembled, with the blessing of Hymen and the Duke.

Table 5 — The Story of Duke Senior

Stage (Element)	Act, Scene	Duke Senior's story
EARTH	II, i	The banished Duke and his company discuss life in the forest. Jaques' lament for a wounded deer is reported to the Duke.
WATER	II, i	The Duke desires immediately to join Jaques, to learn more matter.
AIR	II, vii.	The Duke and his followers are about to eat their picnic. Jaques joins them late, excited at having met a fool in the forest and explaining how he would like to be a fool.
	II, vii.	Orlando rushes upon them, demanding food at sword-point. The Duke courteously invites him and Adam to join the feast.
	II, vii.	Whilst he leaves to fetch Adam, the Duke and Jaques make observations about their state and that of the world and mankind.
	★	The Duke meets Rosalind disguised as Ganymede but doesn't realise she is his daughter, and she in turn does not reveal herself.
FIRE	V, iv	The Duke and his attendant lords all assemble for the magic and the marriages.
	V, iv	Hymen, god of marriage, is conjured up. Rosalind and Celia appear as their true selves. The Duke is reunited with his lost daughter. The eight couples—Rosalind and Orlando, Celia and Oliver, Touchstone and Audrey, Phebe and Silvius—are married with the blessing of Hymen and the Duke.

FIRE (contd)	V, iv	Jaques de Boys arrives and announces that Duke Frederick has been converted to a religious life, and that he surrenders the dukedom to his elder brother and restores all confiscated lands and property to the exiled lords.
	V, iv	The Duke calls on all to complete the marriage celebrations, after which he will share his fortune with all, according to their measure, and return to court to rule.

Table 6 — The Story of Duke Frederick

Stage (Element)	Act, Scene	Duke Frederick's story
EARTH	I, ii	Duke Frederick presides at the wrestling match.
WATER	I, ii	Duke Frederick is incensed against Orlando, refusing to give him the prize.
AIR	I, iii III, i	Duke Frederick banishes Rosalind. Duke Frederick orders Oliver to find Orlando and bring him back, dead or alive.
FIRE	★	Duke Frederick, marching with an army into the forest in order to do battle with his brother, meets a religious man and is converted to a religious life. He surrenders the dukedom to his elder brother and restores all confiscated lands and property to the exiled lords.

6. A Walk through the Heavens

An Alchemical Work

The sequence of eight minor cycles which Shakespeare has used for the story of *As You Like It* takes us and the characters of the play on a walk, as it were, through the planetary heavens. We start on the Earth; then, leaving the Earth, we journey through the spheres of the Moon, Mercury, Venus, Mars, Jupiter, Saturn, until we reach the Sun, the realm of light. Gradually, as we come nearer to the Sun, things get better, although no one actually knows this for certain until the Sun sphere is reached. When it is reached, the resultant harmony and joy, and even material reward, is far beyond what any person could have imagined or expected, for the divine world bestows its blessings in an abundance on all those who strive in friendship for the best.

The general rule seems to be: offer the best of what you have to the Divine, in love and devotion, and the Divine will not only accept that offering but return it to you blessed and magnified many times over. However, we first have to make the offering, and the worthiest offering is, of course, ourselves. Moreover, such offerings have to be real—they have to be personal sacrifices. All those in the play who are blessed in such a way have offered themselves, their lives, as living sacrifices in one way or another. Each is blessed according to his or her deserts—a law which the Duke imitates when he makes his own expression of generosity (V, iv, 171-174):

> *Duke Senior.* And after, every of this happy number
>   That have endur'd shrewd days and nights with us,
>   Shall share the good of our returned fortune,
>   According to the measure of their states.

The result achieved in the Sun sphere is a state of affairs totally different from the original corrupt condition that existed in the beginning, on 'Earth'. A complete transformation and transmutation has taken place. Transformation is a change from one form of expression to another, just as a lit candle transforms from solid to liquid to vapour to flame, or as a plant metamorphoses from seed to shoot to leaf to flower to fruit. Transmutation, on the other hand, is something more than this. It is a raising of one mutable form of life into a higher expression of life, such as the candle does when it becomes light, or the plant does when its fruit is eaten by an animal or human being, thereby becoming part of the body of the higher life form.

This walk, then, through the planetary spheres, is an alchemical work: a pilgrimage which transforms people and ultimately raises them, through transmutation, to a higher level of consciousness and expression of life. Moreover, in all this, nature takes part. The forest provides the setting and the animals participate in the action. As Shakespeare portrays clearly in this play, mankind and nature are not separate from each other but mutually dependant and interconnected.

So it is with the intelligencies of the so-called planetary spheres, the angels of the heavens. In Hermetic and Cabalistic lore, the planets are but symbols of these great spirits which constitute the realm of cosmic intelligence, with its laws and qualities and purposes, and which are inseparable from human life and destiny. We follow those laws because we have to—that is how the universe is designed; but we do have the choice as to the moral level of life on which to express and experience them. We may not always know that they are there, or even believe in them, but that makes no difference to their existence and influence. Like Shakespeare's hidden structures and meanings, they exist, they are powerful, but they remain concealed until we wish to acknowledge and see them. When invoked or looked for, however, they appear; and they can always be called upon for assistance, according to the sphere of action to which they belong.

Hymen

For this reason it is Hymen, god (or spirit) of marriage, who is invoked for the wedding of the four couples: and it is Hymen, son of Apollo (or of Bacchus and Venus), who appears for the purpose and carries out what is needed (V, iv, 107-145).

Fortune & Nature

The goddess Fortune is the subject of a discussion between Rosalind and Celia when they first come on stage at the beginning of the play (I, ii, 30-53). Fortune is the great spirit who turns the Wheel of Fortune, creating the cycles of time with their process of life that take each of us through our transformations and evolutionary changes. The princesses compare her with Nature, whose domain lies in the 'lineaments of nature' whereas Fortune 'reigns in gifts of the world'. That is to say, Nature provides the outer, physical form, the 'Wheel'; Fortune bestows the inner form or psychological life process that animates and turns the Wheel. Nature builds our bodies, Fortune moulds our souls. It is a subtle but important distinction.

> *Ros*. What shall be our sport then?
>
> *Celia*. Let us sit and mock the good hussif Fortune from her wheel, that her gifts may be bestowed equally.
>
> *Ros*. I would we could do so; for her benefits are mightily misplaced, and the bountiful blind woman doth most mistake in her gifts to women.
>
> *Celia*. 'Tis true, for those that she makes fair, she scarce makes honest; and those that she makes honest, she makes very ill-favouredly.
>
> *Ros*. Nay now thou goest from Fortune's office to Nature's; Fortune reigns in gifts of the world, not in the lineaments of Nature.
>
> *Celia*. No? When Nature hath made a fair creature, may she not by Fortune fall into the fire? Though Nature hath given us wit to flout at Fortune, hath not Fortune sent in this fool to cut off the argument? [*Enter Touchstone*]
>
> *Ros*. Indeed, there is Fortune too hard for Nature, when Fortune makes Nature's natural the cutter-off of Nature's wit.
>
> *Celia*. Peradventure this is not Fortune's work neither, but Nature's, who perceiveth our natural wits too dull to reason of such goddesses, and hath sent this natural for our whetstone; for always the dullness of the fool is the whetstone of the wits.

Cupid (Sun)

A little later, seeing her friend stricken with love for Orlando as well as upset about her father's banishment,

Celia calls upon Cupid for mercy ('Cupid have mercy, not a word?' – I, iii, 1). The two princesses then present another of the many exquisite pearls of wisdom, hidden in deliberately ambiguous, metaphorical speech, which Shakespeare has carefully scattered throughout his plays (see Ch. 7).

Cupid is the Roman name for the god of love, the 'First-Born' and Creator of all else, known to the Greeks as Eros ('Love'), Logos ('Word') and Phanes ('Light'), which names correspond to the three degrees of manifestation (*i.e.* desire, thought, action).[25] He is also equated with the Divine Mercury (Greek, Hermes), whose name is derived from the Egyptian *Maa Kheru*, meaning 'True Word'. This is the elder Cupid, the eldest and parent of all the gods and goddesses, according to the Orphic cosmogony, except for Chaos which is neither a god or goddess but the pure, formless, unmanifest Origin and Womb of all things—the 'No-thing' which Hamlet thinks on and fears.[26] There is also a younger Cupid, the youngest of the gods, on whom the attributes of the elder Cupid are bestowed, which relates to the love in each person's heart. However, it is the elder Cupid whom Celia addresses, the Universal Love and Light, whose bride is Psyche, the human soul, the emblem of whom is the rose. Mercy is but one attribute of Cupid, howbeit a major one, which is signified by Jupiter.

Jupiter & Juno

When the two princesses reach the Forest of Arden, Rosalind cries out, 'O Jupiter, how weary are my spirits!' (II, iv, 1). It is more of an exclamation than a conversation or request for help. We might call it swearing, which it probably is. Jupiter (from Latin *Iu-Pater*, meaning 'Father of Light') is the Greek Zeus, from which name is derived the Latin *Deus*, 'God'. Clearly, we still use the same oath! Jupiter is a good aspect of Deity to call upon for help, since he is the Spirit of Mercy. Since help does come immediately to the fatigued women, in the form of Corin, the shepherd, it would appear that Rosalind has a good working relationship with the great god and that he not only hears her cry but responds at once.

Rosalind clearly likes Jupiter, as she often calls upon him—another instance being when she comments on one of Orlando's love-poems, 'O most gentle Jupiter, what tedious homily of love have you wearied your parishioners withal…!' (III, ii, 152-154). In this she attributes the source of the poetry to Jupiter, as the inspirer or muse of the love-sick poet. She is happy when told by Celia that she found Orlando lying under an oak 'like a dropped acorn', for an oak is sacred to Jupiter and therefore, for Rosalind, 'may well be called Jove's tree, when it drops such fruit' (III, ii, 230-233). Jove is an alternative form of Jupiter's name, used also by Rosalind when she witnesses Silvius' passion for Phebe (II, iv, 57).

Rosalind's special connection to Jupiter is highlighted by her choice of Ganymede for her disguise. Ganymede was beloved by Jupiter and taken up by the mighty god into heaven, to become his cup-bearer. Her (and Celia's) close relationship with Jupiter is explained by Celia in the first act of the play, when she describes herself and Rosalind as being 'like Juno's swans' (I, iii, 72). Juno is Jupiter's sister and spouse. This great goddess, queen of the heavens, is acknowledged first in the wedlock song, for 'wedding is great Juno's crown' (V, iv, 140). The swan is not known particularly as an attribute of Juno (a peacock is her best known emblem), but Jupiter took the form of a swan in order to lie with Leda, and a pair of swans pull the solar chariots of Venus and

Apollo. In Christian symbolism, the white swan signifies purity and grace, and is an emblem of the Virgin Mary.

Diana (Moon)

Orlando, by contrast, calls upon Diana, 'thrice-crowned queen of night', to witness his love and survey her 'huntress' name' which he has written in his love verses (III, ii, 1-5). In doing this, he associates Rosalind with the goddess Diana, the divine huntress and daughter of Jupiter, whom the Greeks referred to as the virgin goddess Artemis. Diana is the goddess of light associated with the Moon (*i.e.* the reflected light, equated with intelligence). Her male counterpart is Dianus, better known as Janus, the god of light associated with the Sun (*i.e.* the radiant light, equated with wisdom). Janus is the Greek Apollo, the twin-brother of Artemis.

Diana-Artemis is especially renowned as the goddess of the flocks and the chase—of shepherds and hunters, and of sheep and deer. She is also the goddess of nymphs and is reputed to have hunted with them in the mountains of Arcadia, in the Golden Age, riding in a chariot drawn by four stags with golden antlers.

Saturn

Saturn is also brought into the picture, as Time (II, ii, 297-327), whom Rosalind, disguised as Ganymede, describes wittily and with hidden wisdom to Orlando (see Chapter 7). She refers to Time later as 'the old justice that examines all such offenders' (IV, i, 189-190), for Saturn is the great Spirit that tests and initiates us all, who is said to hold the keys of heaven as its Doorkeeper.[27] Saturn signifies the last sphere through which we have to traverse before we can enter into the blissful light of the Sun; although, of course, the great Time Lord is ever present, watching over us at all times.

Qualities of the Seven Planetary Spirits

As you can see, four of the seven great Planetary Spirits or Archangels (Sun, Moon, Jupiter, Saturn) are mentioned in the text, recognised and called upon quite naturally by the characters of the play. The other three, not directly mentioned, are the great Spirits of Mercury, Venus and Mars, but their influences are definitely present. The Earth is represented by the great goddess Nature.

To understand the cycles or sections of the play better, a description of the relevant qualities and characteristics associated with each Spirit might help. The following is a brief summary, given purely as a rough guide, drawn from the Neoplatonic (*i.e.* Hermetic, Magian and Cabalistic) tradition:

1. Earth   The Kingdom.

2. Moon   Sphere of Generation. The bringer of change, mutability. Associated with the infant.

3. Mercury   Sphere of Thought, Communication – the lower mind or intellect. Associated with the student and the quick-witted person, but also with the trickster and the fool.

4. Venus   Sphere of Emotion, Passion, Friendship – the lower desires and emotions. Associated with the lover, but also with lust.

5. Mars   Sphere of Thought, Perception, Judgment, Severity – the higher mind or intellect. Associated with the warrior and judge, but also with the harsh critic.

6. Jupiter   Sphere of Mercy, Grace, Compassion, Benevolence, Generosity, Charity, Self-Sacrifice – the higher emotions. Associated with the 'justice'—the high authority, the king, the teacher, the wise person, the guru, the saviour (*i.e.* 'saving grace').

7. Saturn   Sphere of Knowledge and Partial Revelation, and of Guardianship and Testing. Associated with the 'pantaloon' or old age, but also with the wise and knowledgeable, the magus or magician. Saturn is the gatekeeper and gateway to the Sun Sphere.

8. Sun.   Sphere of Love, Harmony, Beauty, Marriage, Union, Full Revelation and Joy. This is the place of the heart, the real source of love and light and life—the Seat of Divinity, the Place of Truth, the mystic Sun-Rose.

Cycle 1 (Earth)

The play begins, literally and symbolically, right at the very beginning, with Orlando and Adam conversing together in an orchard. This couldn't be a clearer analogy with the Garden of Eden. Even the fact that Orlando has been fed with the 'hinds' (which has the ambiguous meaning of either female deer or farm-servants) and kept no different from the 'stalling of an ox', and that he is fed up with this situation and wants to leave it, is a kind of witty, perhaps irreverent, parody of Adam and Eve's predicament in the original Orchard of Eden.

Orlando has eaten the apple, sees he is naked, and wants something that he thinks is his right to have, but which is kept from him. It is, indeed, his liberty and inheritance that he wants. So he leaves the 'Eden', chased out under dire threat of death, just as Adam and Eve were chased out. The underlying reason, however, for this seeming disaster, is so that he might, symbolically speaking, eat of the tree of life and gain his freedom. Since the word *freedom* is derived from the Sanskrit root *pri*, meaning 'to love', what Orlando is seeking, and which he finds, is a state of love. This love is indeed life in the truest sense, and is the crown and illumination of all human endeavour. Like in the Bible, this crown of love is achieved only at the end of the play: for the tree of life is life itself, with all its adventures and challenges. To gain its fruit this tree must be climbed step by step until, at the end, its very heart is found, wherein the golden prize of love grows.

As yet, however, in this first section or cycle of the play, Orlando has not even thought about leaving his home territory, but he wants change. He wants to remedy the situation but doesn't know how to. He then precipitates a situation where the change is actually forced upon him. His prayer has been heard, although he has no way of knowing, at that early stage, of how it is being answered.

Orlando precipitates his exile and all that follows through wrestling, first with his brother and then with

Charles, Duke Frederick's champion, and winning. It is a fact of life that those who are in positions of power and authority through the actual abuse of their power and authority, are dreadfully afraid of anyone who appears to be able to challenge them in terms of strength and will-power, and more especially if they have virtue. The classic biblical example, relevant to this story since the play begins with a scriptural parody, is that of Jesus of Nazareth. Orlando demonstrates quite clearly that he is a threat to both Oliver and Duke Frederick, and therefore must die.

In such a situation nothing virtuous can remain in either the court or the De Boys house, for the tyrants are casting all virtue out. Therefore the feminine embodiments of virtue—Rosalind and Celia—must also go. However, because they leave the court and city, and Orlando likewise leaves, the prospective lovers have the opportunity to come together in love and marriage in a way that would have been impossible had they stayed. Moreover, the corruptness of the court and society has the chance of being purified and changed by their own leap into the dark.

This first section sets the scene of the story. It provides the impulse that gets things going: but the actual action proper begins in the next section, the Moon cycle.

Cycle 2 (Moon)

In this second section of the play, the Moon cycle, both Orlando and Adam on the one hand, and also the two princesses with Touchstone on the other hand, leave their homes for the Forest of Arden. In terms of the staged drama, we do not witness the ladies departing, although we know that they are about to do so at the end of the first section, and in the third section we find that they have done so. Orlando, however, we are shown deciding to flee, and leaving with his servant, Adam. Added to this, there is the strange but deeply significant scene of the banished Duke in the forest, who hears of Jaques' sorrowing for a wounded deer and immediately desires to leave where he is in order to join Jaques. His reason is that he enjoys the 'matter' which Jaques deliberates upon, melancholy being the first stage leading to deep insights and real knowledge. The Duke is keen to learn all he can from nature and people.

These exoduses are the birth point of the play—the first movements that occur after the initial impulse has been given. In this section all the key characters are moving into new positions, like babies being born from their wombs. This is a generative activity, governed by the Moon. The lunar aspect of this cycle is further emphasised by the wounded deer, with which Jaques sympathises. The deer is a sacred animal to Diana (Artemis), the goddess of the Moon; who, although she is goddess of the hunt, hates to see or feel her animals in pain. Such agony is the result of bad or inaccurate hunting. A true hunter, who is like a shaman or a master of Zen, never misses the kill. The Duke must talk with Jaques, to learn why his hunters missed their aim and how they should do better.

The deer is a symbol of the heart, hence its alternative name is hart, and a loved person is a dear person. A heart shot through with an arrow represents love and loving. Such love requires self-sacrifice—an offering of oneself, one's heart. The animals in the play reflect and symbolise the actions of human beings, just as happens in our real world. Nature always speaks a language to us. If we hurt each other, nature is also hurt—and, moreover, nature shows us symbolically where the hurt has occurred, like a mirror. This is a truth that Shakespeare knows well, for he has clearly studied both nature and the human being most profoundly.

Cycle 3 (Mercury)

The third cycle of the play begins with Rosalind and Celia meeting the shepherds and arranging to buy a cottage, some pasture land and a flock of sheep. In doing this they are acting intelligently, with initiative, and organising a home and means of living for themselves so that they might survive in the forest. Corin, the shepherd, who fortuitously meets them just at the right moment, with both the news of the property for sale and the ability to arrange it for the princesses, is for them a remarkable messenger, sent by heaven (Jupiter) in answer to their prayers.

Just as the symbolic story of Adam and the Orchard was placed in the first part of the first cycle, and the story of the wounded deer was placed in the first part of the second cycle, so this story of the shepherd-messenger is in the first part of this third cycle. The god Mercury, known to the Greeks as Hermes, is commonly represented as a shepherd. In his highest sense, he is the Pymander, 'the Shepherd of Men', the 'good shepherd' who is the *Nous*, the Mind and Light of the Supreme.[28] Hermes is, in this instance, the Pymander's pupil, known as Hermes Trismegistus ('the thrice greatest'), who becomes the representative and embodiment (or 'likeness') of the divine Pymander on earth. In the planetary sense, however, Mercury is but an aspect of the Pymander, to do with thought and communication; but there is a key to the mystery of divine light and the human being in this

Mercurial aspect. For instance, *man* means 'the mind' or 'thinker', and is created in the 'likeness' or 'image' of God.[29] The episode of the shepherd Corin, and the purchasing of the cottage and flock of sheep, is a highly significant allegory pertaining to the mysterious heart and purpose of humanity. (See Chapter 8)

The remainder of this third cycle dwells mainly on themes of thinking, observation, explanations and storytelling. It is epitomised by Jaques' excitement at meeting a professional fool in the forest, and his eagerness to explain to the Duke and his entourage why he would like to be a fool. His explanation comes close to the Classical ideal of a human being, a Hermes figure, who is able to speak his mind and 'cleanse the foul body of th'infected world': for the good shepherd is also a healer and teacher of mankind.

The fool is likewise a symbol of Mercury, invested in his motley disguise, able to be all things to all people, in this world but not of this world, and capable of rising to the heights of heaven and descending into the depths of the earth or underworld, freely, as a messenger and guide to help others. The really great fool is genuinely mercurial, and able to be both happy and sad, jovial and melancholic, shallow and deep, petty and meaningful, all at the same time. The wise fool teaches through entertainment. The matters of which such a fool speaks can be taken 'as you like it', which is why the professional fool, once known as the jester or troubadour in medieval times and as the bard in the Celtic period, had licence to roam whither he would and to speak whatever he wished, under the traditional protection of all those in authority. No one was ever to harm a fool and all were to provide for his needs as required. In return, he was expected to be proficient in his art and temperate in his behaviour—which is why the Duke ridicules Jaques' desire to become a fool, for Jaques had been a libertine (II, vii, 65-69). Moreover, Jaques' temperament is almost solely melancholic and satirical: he has not yet acquired the necessary good humour needed to uplift and help others.

The fool, like the shepherd, is the key to this section and to the hidden meaning of the play. It is also a key to Shakespeare, the great English bard.

Cycle 4 (Venus)

The fourth, Venusian cycle begins with Orlando wandering through the forest and hanging love poems on the trees. Love-making lies especially in the domain of Venus, the Aphrodite of the Greeks. Orlando writes the poetry to his love, Rosalind, whom he adulates like a goddess. The rose, the name of which is the principal part of Rosalind's name, is not only the symbol of love but is especially the emblem of Venus-Aphrodite. Once again, Shakespeare begins a section of the play with the appropriate symbolism for that cycle.

The whole of this cycle concerns love and love-making, and the curing of love-sickness. The emotional (*water*) part of the cycle has Rosalind displaying such emotion that she is angry. The thinking (*air*) part of the cycle starts with Celia revealing to Rosalind that she has discovered her lover in the forest, under an oak (the tree of the great god of compassionate love), and continues with the two princesses watching and listening to Orlando and Jaques arguing about the love poems. It culminates with Rosalind, as Ganymede, explaining to Orlando that she can cure his love-sickness. The fourth (*fire*) part of the cycle shows the fool, Touchstone, attempting to marry Audrey in the woods, privately, until persuaded by Jaques that the marriage should be done better. In this,

Jaques is a genuine help and, moreover, to the fool who this time is in need of help.

Cycle 5 (Mars)

The fifth cycle of the play opens with Rosalind revealing to Celia that she has met her father, but that he did not recognise her in her disguise. From this sharing of information, the princesses, invited by Corin the shepherd, go on to witness the courtship of Phebe by Silvius.

Seeing, witnessing, judging matters in order to recognise, understand and know, is the role ascribed to Mars. The Duke saw but did not see his daughter, Rosalind. He saw her mask, her disguise, and believed it. His intuition in this was not as strong as his intellect. Mars is more to do with the eye of the mind or intellect than the eye of the heart. It has its limitations, and often sets limitations by dogmatising its ideas and perceptions of how it sees truth. As an analyser, which separates one thing apart from another in order to make comparisons, it is like a judge with a flaming sword, a warrior seeking for and zealously guarding truth in the form that he sees it.

This comparison and judgmental aspect is brought out in the second, third and fourth parts of this martial cycle. In the second part Rosalind considers Phebe wrong to treat Silvius the way she does and, in her anger, castigates the shepherdess. Then, in the third part, when discussing melancholy with Jaques, she disagrees with Jaques' point of view. Warrior-like, she derides Jaques for selling his lands in order to travel in search of what she considers to be vain knowledge. When Orlando finally arrives, in the last part of this section, she berates him for being late.

The culmination of the fourth part of this section concerns the start of the love-cure, which requires a great sacrifice of her own desires on Rosalind's part, and the maintenance of her disguise, which leads on into a mock marriage. Like the Duke, Rosalind's father, Orlando does not recognise his love in her disguise; and so the marriage is illusory, although it could have been real if he had only been able to see clearly. As he takes his leave, Rosalind remarks pertinently: 'Well, Time is the old justice that examines all such offenders, and let Time try' (IV, i, 189-190).

Then it is Rosalind's turn to be castigated by her friend Celia, for misusing her sex in her love-prate. Rosalind responds, exclaiming if only Celia knew (*i.e.* could see) how deep she is in love, but the bottom of her love is too deep to be seen. Celia, half-jestingly, disagrees, suggesting that from her point of view Rosalind's love is bottomless in the sense that as fast as affection is poured in, it runs out. Indignant, Rosalind replies with another exquisitely accurate and meaningful statement appropriate to the spirit of this cycle (IV, i, 201-end):

> Ros. No. That same bastard of Venus, that was begot of thought, conceived of spleen and born of madness, that rascally boy that abuses everyone's eyes because his own are out, let him be judge how deep I am in love. I'll tell thee Aliena, I cannot be out of the sight of Orlando. I'll go and find a shadow and sigh till he come.
>
> *Celia.* And I'll sleep.

In this section we are dealing with semi-truths and illusions, shadows, dreams and blindness, although the role of the intellect is, ultimately, to see clearly in order to understand. But the eye of the mind needs the compassionate and intuitive love of the heart to enable it to see all truth, and this stage of initiation is yet to come. We have to move from an academic perception to the truer mystery of the heart, disguised behind further veils which we have to learn to draw open.

Cycle 6 (Jupiter)

That which uncovers the mystery is charity, which is loving self-sacrifice for the good of others. The sixth cycle of the play is governed by Jupiter, the Spirit of Mercy, whose actions are charitable. It begins with a sacrifice—the killing of a deer, which this time is done properly and celebrated accordingly. Nature here echoes what takes place in the realm of humanity: and indeed two sacrifices take place: Orlando's in risking his life to save Oliver's, and Oliver who dies to his old style of 'brute' behaviour in order to be born into a new and better way of life.

A third type of death also takes place, in the fourth (*fire*) part of this section, when Rosalind is given the bloody napkin which had bound Orlando's wound. She swoons at the sight of the blood, in an intuitive sympathy with the hurt received by her lover and beloved. Blood is a symbol of the heart and especially of compassion—of love poured out for others. The Christian iconography of the pelican piercing its breast, in order to feed its young with the blood that issues from its heart, is an example of this compassion and self-sacrifice. Likewise, the grail cup filled with the blood of Christ is symbolic of this mercy, this grace of love. The cup is not only filled but shared with others that they might also drink of the mercy. Such a sharing enables each of us, by symbiosis and assimilation, to be partakers in this love and the consciousness of this love.

The bloody napkin is a kind of grail, sent by Orlando to his beloved Rosalind. Partaking of its essence (*i.e.* the love that lies behind the outer form), Rosalind faints and briefly enters another state of consciousness. When she

returns to her more normal awareness, she expresses the
wish to be at home. Home is where the heart is. Oliver
instinctively points out that she lacks a man's heart,
which is, of course, true. It is a man's heart she wants, the
place where she will feel at home, for her woman's heart
is there already. She tries to tell Oliver that her faint was a
counterfeit, but Oliver sees clearly that it was 'a passion of
earnest'. He sees the truth. She still persists, and so Oliver,
kindly, says, 'Well then, take a good heart, and counterfeit
to be a man' (iv, iii, 173-4).

Cycle 7 (Saturn)

The Saturn cycle is a testing time, a waiting time, a time of
expectation rather than of complete fulfilment. In it all the
threads of the story are brought to a head, but there has
to be a waiting period before the final completion can be
celebrated. Saturn is ruler of the Sabbath, the time of
peace. It is indeed a period of peace, and of knowledge
which accompanies the peace, yet it is only the foretaste
of the real illumination and joy that is about to dawn.
Saturn's particular illumination is rather a clarity of situation
and purpose than a dawning light. It is said in folklore
that the darkest time is immediately before dawn, and
this is also the time of greatest clarity. Such is Saturn, for
he is followed by the Sun, just as Saturday (the Sabbath)
is followed by Sunday (the Day of Light). Saturn is the
Doorkeeper of heaven. We have to wait with him, and be
examined by him, before we can enter through the door
into a greater light. If we are not fitted to partake of the
joys awaiting the other side of the door, then our way is
barred, for Saturn guards the gate and makes certain that
only those who are worthy and right for the greater experience pass through the doorway.

The very first action of Saturn is to chase off those not ready or right for the particular Sun experience offered. Therefore, in the first part of this Saturnian cycle, William is seen off by Touchstone, for it is Touchstone who will marry Audrey, according to both Audrey and Touchstone's wishes, and not William. They are both clear on this matter. So are Oliver and Celia concerning their intention to marry, and this Oliver makes clear to his brother, Orlando.

Saturn is the supreme judge of our karma, who ensures that all rights are wronged. In sacred tradition he is referred to as the Angel of the Last Judgement, who reads our karma and decides what is good and what is not good. He uses his 'keys' like sceptres or rods of power to send the good one way and the bad the other, or to send what is appropriate to where it belongs. He demands humility and balances all things, for only what is truly humble and balanced can go through the door to the Sun.

This humbling and balancing occurs with Oliver, who promises to surrender to Orlando possession of the family house together with the revenue that belongs with it. In this way, Oliver makes amends. It is materially more than Sir Rowland de Boys had bequeathed to Orlando, but it makes reparation for the education and upbringing that Oliver denied his youngest brother.

In addition, Oliver asks Orlando for his consent in his marriage to Aliena. This is an expression of friendship and humility, and respect for family and social ties. It acknowledges the importance and adulthood of his youngest brother, for whom Oliver was made responsible *in loco parentis.* Orlando, in his turn, gives his consent and more, promising to organise a great wedding on the morrow, with the Duke and all his company attending.

A Walk through the Heavens

Orlando, knowing now exactly what his heart wants the most, and that his love for Rosalind is real and serious, makes it clear to Ganymede that he cannot continue with the love-cure. Its effect has been to test his love and even increase it, and, now that he sees his brother's love and happiness with Aliena, he knows absolutely clearly that this is what he wants with Rosalind. However, he does not believe it possible. For him, the cup is bitter—or so he thinks. Indeed, he believes he can 'no longer live by thinking' (V, ii, 50).

Rosalind, as Ganymede, immediately responds with her declaration that she can work magic. The thinking has stopped and the action (*i.e.* the *fire* stage of this cycle) has begun. With crystal clarity she knows what to do and she does it. She is a magician, inspired, and so she begins her magic there and then by convincing Orlando and the others that she can do what she claims and bring about a happy ending for all. Saturn is known as the great magician. He is equated with Pan, the Spirit of Nature as well as being the Lord of Time and Space. Like Krishna, Pan can mould nature, including the circumstances of human beings, to the sound of his pipes. All magic is created through sound.

Appropriately, therefore, the culmination of this Saturnian cycle is with an oath and a song. The oath is set against the possibility of dying: but, interestingly, the usual way of speaking this oath is turned around, with deep and positive significance (V, iii, 123-end):

> *Silvius.* I'll not fail, if I live.
> *Phebe.* Nor I.
> *Orlando.* Nor I.

The song is given by two pages, at the request of Touchstone, and is a pretty love song concerning two 'sweet lovers' who love the spring. Aware of the greater harmony that is yet to come, Touchstone complains about the singing, which turns into a jest concerning time and 'lost truth which is brought forth by time':

> *First Page.* You are deceived sir. We kept time, we lost not our time.
>
> *Touchstone.* By my troth yes. I count it but time lost to hear such a foolish song. God buy you, and God mend your voices. Come Audrey.

Cycle 8 (Sun)

The final cycle is that of the Sun, towards which all the other minor 'planetary' cycles have been leading, as steps on the way. The great Spirits of the Sun are Apollo and, at a deeper level, the Pymander, the Divine Mercury or Christos, known also to the Greeks as Eros and to the Romans as Cupid: but in fact all gods and goddesses, all angels, all spirits, belong to this one universal light of love, as aspects of the light. Like the physical sun, the spiritual Sun is central to all else in its solar system, and all else is derived from this Sun and lives in its light. Although it appears that it is the goal at the end of the journey—the crown of the mountain or the top rung of the ladder—it is in fact the heart. The rest is an illusion.

The central character of the whole play is Rosalind, sought for by her lover, Orlando the hero. Her name signifies the heart and all that that means, for the rose is the emblem of love and of the heart. It signifies balance and harmony; but, more especially, beauty. Beauty is the flower of harmony. Beauty was personified in the Greek Mysteries by Persephone, the daughter of Demeter; whilst Demeter herself signified harmony. Persephone was known as the 'lost one' (*c.f.* Perdita, 'the lost one', whose mother is Hermione, 'Harmony', in Shakespeare's *Winter's Tale*). The rose is Persephone's symbol. She further signifies the truth which is lost by being hidden in matter, or nature, and has to be found. The 'Lost Word' of the Freemasons is likewise equated with this mystery and beauty of love.

Orlando achieves Rosalind in marriage only when he has reached the heart, the Sun; for only in the Sun, the heart, are all things resolved and married together in union. The other three couples, also, are married in the Sun sphere, for this is the only place for a true and blessed union. As Hymen says (V, iv, 107-109):

> Then there is mirth in heaven
> When earthly things made even
> Atone together.

The particular spirit or god of marriage was known to the Greeks and Romans as Hymen (or Hymenaeus), the son of Apollo. He was envisioned as an extraordinarily beautiful youth, who was a Muse and who was invoked in the bridal song, originally known as the hymeneal song. In fact, his name originally designated the song itself. That is to say, he is the song—for the essence of all gods, the archetypes of the universe, is sound. Hymen's form is but the imaginative picture of the song or sound. For these reasons there is music when Hymen appears (as also when any god or goddess appears in the Shakespeare plays), which culminates in the 'wedlock hymn'.

Significantly, the number of persons who are joined in marriage, as four couples, is associated with the symbolism of the heart. '8' is particularly the number of the Holy Spirit and of the divine Mercury. The blood flow, associated with the heart and with both love and life, flows through the body in a figure-of-eight. The '8' is still used today in mathematics as the cosmic lemniscate, the sign for infinity.

In Egyptian cosmology, the primary source of the Hermetic wisdom, the 'Eight' relates to the creation myth of Hermopolis, 'City of Hermes', the heart centre of ancient Egypt. Hermes is the Greek name for the Egyptian Thoth, 'lord of divine words', the personification of Wisdom, who taught humanity the wisdom and science of creation. Thoth is in fact the Word, the 'heart and tongue' of Ra, the Light, who spoke the words which expressed the divine Will and resulted in the creation of the cosmos.[30] An earlier name for Thoth's city was Khmun or Khemenu, meaning 'City of the Eight', or Un, 'Pure Existence', which also has the meaning of 'One' or 'Unity'.

The Hermopolitan creation myth recounts how the Ogdoad or Primordial Eight existed as a single potential Entity in the original Nun or Chaos, the primordial ocean of matter. In the Heliopolitan creation myth, this single potential Entity is called Atum—who is male in respect, and only in respect, of Nun, the female aspect of Divinity—whilst in the Hebraic-Christian scriptures he is called 'the Spirit'.[31] Through the projection of his heart (*i.e.* through desire, or loving) Atum came into being within the Nun, composed of the eight principles or qualities represented by the Ogdoad. The Ogdoad were envisioned as four couples, male and female, whose names mean 'the initial waters', 'spatial infinity', 'the darkness' and 'That which is hidden'. As they came into being they formed a light, represented as a child called Rê (Ra). The heart itself (*i.e.* the heart of God, heart of the universe), from which this child was born, was symbolised as a lotus floating on the universal waters.

A Walk through the Heavens

The lotus is the equivalent of the rose, which was substituted for the lotus in later wisdom teachings. The Ogdoad are called the 'fathers and mothers' of the child, whilst the child is the equivalent of the 'jewel in the lotus' of Hindu and Buddhist teachings—the spiritual Sun. The lotus or rose signifies the beauty of the Sun-child, whilst the light is its radiant joy.

Floating on the waters of life, the lotus is also the ark in which the child of light dwells, like the child Moses in his ark of bulrushes, or the poet Taliesin in his coracle, or Noah in his ark that floated upon the waters of the Flood. This concept is introduced by Jaques in the last scene, as the couples enter ready for their marriage: 'There is sure another flood toward, and these couples are coming to the ark' (V, iv, 35-36). In the story of the Flood, four human couples are saved by being taken into the ark: namely, Noah and his three sons, together with their wives.[32]

This idea of the unmanifest One that manifests itself by means of its eight divine qualities or principles, paired as four couples,[33] is inherent in all four of the main Egyptian creation myths: the other three—at Memphis, Heliopolis and Thebes—being extensions of the Hermopolitan heart creation. The philosophical and mathematical formula of all this is enshrined in the famous lines inscribed on the coffin of Petamon, now in the Cairo museum:

I am One that transforms into Two
I am Two that transforms into Four
I am Four that transforms into Eight
After this I am One.[34]

This One, the 'child' that is Light, having come into existence, was seen by God (Atum) as being 'good'.[35] In the Hebrew text of *Genesis*, 'good' has the meaning of 'beautiful', as in the related Hebrew text of *Ecclesiastes* which says:

> He [God] hath made everything beautiful in his time [*i.e.* proper season]: also he hath set the world in their heart, so that no man can find out the work that God maketh from the beginning to the end.[36]

This same biblical text continues with lines that sum up this Sun cycle of Shakespeare's play, and the whole play itself:

> I know that there is no good in them, but for a man to rejoice, and to do good in his life.

> And also that every man should eat and drink, and enjoy the good of all his labour, it is the gift of God.[37]

Thus it is that this cycle, and the play, ends with enjoyment—the celebration of the marriages and all the preceding labour. 'First in this forest,' says the Duke to Jaques de Boys, 'let us do those ends that here were well begun and well begot…. Play music, and you brides and bridegrooms all, with measure heap'd in joy, to th'measures fall'. Music, dancing and joy go hand in hand, fulfilling the meaning of Protorhythmos ('First of Eurhythmy') as an Orphic title of Eros. Eurhythmy is a graceful, harmonious rhythm, order and movement, or dance, accompanying music which it expresses. It is the dance of creation when 'the Morning Stars sang together'.[38]

The Duke's last words, the final words of the play, are:

> *Duke Sen.* Proceed, proceed. We will begin these rites,
>   As we do trust they'll end, in true delights.

To the memory of my beloued,
The AVTHOR
Mr. William Shakespeare:
And
what he hath left vs.

The Seven-fold Vibration

In the 1st Shakespeare Folio (1623), the title and text of *As You Like It* is headed by a notable headpiece. The design of this headpiece indicates a wave pattern, a seven-fold vibration interwoven with a vine-like natural form, which seems to be an excellent representation in symbolic pictorial form of the seven ages of man and all that that means. To the Freemasonically minded, this pattern is that of seven Masonic Squares, the sign of the seven-fold Master. The same headpiece is printed above Ben Jonson's poetic tribute to Shakespeare, crowning the dedication, 'To the memory of my beloved, The AUTHOR Mr. William Shakespeare: And what he hath left us'.[39]

7. Love's Knowledge

Cupid

Shakespeare was a brilliant master of ambiguity, and of metaphor and allegory. Behind the veil of poetry, humour and Renaissance classicism he is able to convey the deepest truths and philosophy which, spoken openly, could have incurred at the best displeasure and at the worst condemnation as a heretic, with all that that meant. However, this is not the only reason for such 'disguise': Shakespeare is following a very ancient and proven method of teaching, by concealing great truths behind the masks of allegory and drama so that readers and audiences can take it as they like it. Moreover, searching for truth is always a worthwhile task, for the human being has a natural curiosity and hunting instinct, and enjoys the thrill of discovery. For this reason the great masters of wisdom have generally used parable and metaphor when addressing the general public, whilst leaving sign-posts for the interested to follow and explaining truths more openly to those that ask and are ready. A good example of this is in connection with Cupid, the god of love.

A Love Catechism

As has already been seen, the idea and presence of Cupid is a primary feature of *As You Like It* from start to finish.

Cupid's presence is first invoked by Celia at the beginning of the second scene of Act 1, although the question of whether love is present or absent has been a major theme from the start of the play. This invocation of Cupid begins a skilful game of repartee between Celia and Rosalind, pregnant with hidden meaning, like a kind of catechism presented in the form of a jest or play of wit.

Cupid, the god of love, was known to the Greek and Orphic philosophers as the greatest of all gods, the first-born and creator of all else that exists. Since he was known to the Greeks as both Eros and Logos, 'the Word', by means of which all chaotic matter is brought together and organised into an ordered harmony or cosmos, it is not by chance that Celia follows up her invocation with a pun on 'word', and Rosalind responds with a suitable pun on 'dog' (I, iii, 1-3):

> *Celia.* Why cousin, why Rosalind! Cupid have mercy, not a word?
> *Ros.* Not one to throw at a dog.

'Dog' is a synonym for 'God' spelt backwards, which implies the opposite of God. Since Cupid is a Latin word for Christ, as God the Creator, so 'dog' implies the Anti-Christ. Such 'dogs' are 'curs'—a word-play on 'curse'—as Celia next points out (I, iii, 4-6):

> *Celia.* No, thy words are too precious to be cast away upon curs. Throw some of them at me; come lame me with reasons.

Celia asks to be made lame with reasons. The Logos was known as the Divine Reason or Wisdom of Love, and all true words are wise thoughts or 'reasons' which are presented by the heart to the mind, for the mind to contemplate. The lameness is a subtle reference to Dionysos, whose name means both 'the Divine Son' (or 'Son of God') and 'the Lame God'. Dionysos is the Greek mystery name for Eros (Love), who is also Logos (Word) and Phanes (Light)—the 'First-born' or first, single, complete, universal manifestation of Deity—the Macrocosmic Sun. Celia not only reveals the mystery name of what Christianity calls the Word or Christ, but also reveals the philosophical reason why Dionysos was considered to be lame. Divine love, whose consciousness is fundamentally pure wisdom, is made lame with rational thought, or reason: for thought ties up or even injures love when it tries to rationalise it. Yet, without reason we would be mad, as Rosalind implies (I, iii, 7-9):

> *Ros.* Then there were two cousins laid up, when the one should be lamed with reasons and the other mad without any.

Not only is Rosalind aware of what reason does and how Cupid-Dionysos is made lame, but she also makes the distinction between the passion of love that has no reason and can therefore be 'mad' (*e.g.* such as in an irrational frenzy of love), and the reason which can make that passion of love 'lame' (*e.g.* cool it or slow it down). She further equates the one state of being with herself and the other with her cousin Celia. Passion and reason are natural polarities to each other, sometimes described and paired as affection and reason, compassion and judgment, or wisdom and intelligence. The one is associated with the heart, the other with the mind. Rosalind personifies the more compassionate, affectionate person, who speaks wisdom, whilst Celia represents the more intellectual, perceptive person, who matches Rosalind's wisdom with intelligent understanding and wit. Together they are Shakespeare's representatives of the wisdom and intelligence of the soul, which their names boldly declare (see Chapter 9).

The princesses carry on in this profound philosophical vein, punning on the meaning of what they are referring to, when Celia asks, 'Is this for your father?' and Rosalind replies, 'No, some of it is for my child's father' (I, iii, 10-11). Outwardly, of course, Celia is referring to Rosalind's natural father, the banished Duke, whilst Rosalind refers to the as yet unborn child she hopes for from her future liaison with Orlando. However, inwardly, or spiritually, it is another matter, for the outer is but a symbol of the inner.

Dionysos, or Cupid, according to the Hermetic Wisdom, is the name for the second aspect of Deity, known as the First-Born Son of God. This Son or Sun is the universal manifestation of the first aspect of Deity—the supreme, abstract and unmanifest Power (*i.e.* Potential), known as the Infinite Darkness, of which Light is its first expression. The Hermetic Wisdom, including Judaism and Christianity, refers to these two as the Father and Son. The third aspect is that of the Redeemer, the divine love seeded in the heart of mankind and nature as a microcosmic sun, which is our personal life-bestowing and regenerating principle, which Christianity refers to as the Holy Spirit. This seed can grow like a child, drawing to itself and transmuting matter into light, until the whole person becomes a sun, a light, a redeemer. Such a person is known as a son of the Son (or son of the Sun), a child of Light—the younger Cupid.[40]

The human heart is associated with the human soul, and both are symbolised by the rose. Psyche, the soul, was known to the Greeks as the beloved bride and wife of Cupid, and her symbol was the rose. Therefore, in this ambiguous word-play of Rosalind and Celia, Shakespeare infers that Rosalind, the 'living Rose', is representative of Cupid's bride and the potential mother of the Redeemer.

Giving birth to and raising the sun-child, the Redeemer, is a path that can be strewn with thorns, as symbolised by the seven sorrows of Mary and Jesus' crown of thorns. The devout Simeon put it well when, blessing the child Jesus, he said to Mary: 'Behold, this child is set for the fall and rising again of many in Israel; and for a sign which shall be spoken against; (Yea, a sword will pierce through thine own soul also) that the thoughts of many hearts may be revealed.'[41] The two women refer to this mystery in their following lines (I, iii, 11-17):

> *Ros.* O how full of briars is this working-day world!
> *Celia.* They are but burs, cousin, thrown upon thee in
>   holiday foolery; if we walk not in the trodden paths
>   our very petticoats will catch them.
> *Ros.* I could shake them off my coat: these burs are in
>   my heart.

Celia then suggests an answer to Rosalind's predicament, making an allusion not only to the prickly flower head of the burdock but also to the Sleeping Princess of the fairy tale, hemmed in by a hedge of thorns. They are the thorns of rose bushes (briars) and Rosalind is the rose bud waiting to be kissed and awoken by her Prince. Celia's answer is to 'Hem them away', to which Rosalind replies, 'I would try, if I could cry hem and have him' (I, iii, 18-19). Here Rosalind puns on 'hem' and 'him', again with double meaning. The hem refers to the sound made when clearing the throat of blockages, and is not only a reality in use but also a word-play on 'hum', the human sound that approximates to and represents the sound of the universe as it vibrates in love to the Word of God.

'Hum' is equated with the Hindu and Buddhist sacred sound, 'Aum', and is the Western equivalent of it. 'Hum' is, therefore, a synonym for the Word of God, the Son or Light of Love—the 'him' whom Rosalind loves in her deepest self. Cleverly, the conversation is brought back to the Word of God with which it began, so rounding off a catechism that has followed, stage by stage, the process of creation and evolution of the human soul.

The Cupid Headpiece

Not only is Cupid-Dionysos an essential feature of *As You Like It* and every other play of Shakespeare's, but the god of love is represented visually and prominently four times in the 1st Shakespeare Folio, in the form of a headpiece to *The Dedication* at the beginning of the Folio (immediately after the title page), the *Catalogue* which lists and names the plays in the Folio, *The Tempest* which is the first play printed in the Folio (and reputedly the last completely 'Shakespeare' play to be written), and the strangely isolated *Epilogue* to the *Second Part of King Henry the Fourth*. In this arrangement there is a cabalistic design waiting to be discovered.

The headpiece is a beautifully designed and executed woodcut print, depicting Cupid-Dionysos seated in the centre upon a cornucopia of grapes, his eyes closed in meditation and holding aloft two birds of paradise in his two hands. Symbolic plumes of illumination rise from the crown of his head, and the veil of truth, tied to each shoulder, has fallen from in front of him, revealing his form. Often Shakespeare quotes the common meaning of the closed eyes as being because Cupid is blind, but the deeper meaning is that 'love looks not with the eyes, but with the mind, and therefore is wing'd Cupid painted blind'.[42] Cupid is traditionally depicted as a naked child, 'because in choice he is so oft beguil'd';[43] but when Cupid's mind is developed he sees all and knows all. In particular, Cupid (love) sees truth, which is good and beautiful ('And God saw the light, that it was good')[44], hence the Cupid of the headpiece is shown holding aloft birds of paradise. Birds are symbols of thoughts, naked-ness is representative of truth, and childhood is emblematic of innocence or purity in love, as also of eternal life.

The Cupid of this headpiece is almost certainly intended to be the younger Cupid, who has to grow to become like his father, the elder Cupid. This is indicated by the cornucopia of grapes, which in Orphic tradition represented the 'harvest' sacrifice required of the human soul in order to give birth to the spiritual soul, the Dionysos. Cupid-Dionysos is the wine of the holy grail, whilst the grail itself is the psyche, the human soul. The two Archers each side of the Dionysus figure would appear to be representations of the titanic love forces embodied in nature, whose arrows pierce the heart and which bring about the necessary 'death' initiation that leads to the resurrection or rebirth of the soul as Dionysus.

A good summary and commentary on the Classical myth of Cupid is provided by Francis Bacon, whose *Essays* and *Wisdom of the Ancients* always seem to furnish apt commentaries on the philosophy, design and symbolic language of Shakespeare's plays. About the traditional story and symbolism of Cupid, he records:

> They say then that Love was the most ancient of all the gods; the most ancient therefore of all things whatever, except Chaos, which is said to have been coeval with him; and Chaos is never distinguished by the ancients with divine honour or the name of a god. This Love is introduced without any parent at all; only, that some say he was an egg of Night. And himself out of Chaos begot all things, the gods included. The attributes which are assigned to him are in number four: he is always an infant; he is blind; he is naked; he is an archer. [45]

Pan

Spirit of Nature, Son of Cupid

The Greek philosophers named the son of Cupid, Pan. Pan was known to them, along with Cupid, as the great god of Arcadia, god of shepherds, huntsmen and of all country folk. As mentioned before, he it is who is, primarily, the 'great magician obscured in the circle of this forest', although Pan himself is but the 'image' of the Word of God (*i.e.* his father, Cupid). His circle is the magic circle of time and space, as symbolised by the rings of the planet Saturn and the orbital ring which the planet makes about the sun.

Philosophically, Pan is known as the spirit of Nature—the mind or intelligence of all natural creation which is evolving as the body of Nature evolves, for the two are integral to each other. The outer form of Nature is the body of Pan, its spirit. For this reason, Pan is symbolised as a creature who stands upon the rocky earth, sprouting with vegetation, with the lower part of his body in the form of an animal (a goat) and his upper torso and face being that of a human being. He is bearded and horned, both beard and horn being symbols of wisdom. His horns touch heaven, and he has wings, denoting both his angelic status and his mediatorship between heaven and earth.

In this invented picture, the ancients encapsulated the idea of the creation and evolution of the Cosmos through all its kingdoms of life, with mankind being the final creation and crown of the rest. The symbolic image of Pan is a pictograph of, for instance, the Six Days of Creation as recorded by the prophet Moses in the first chapter of *Genesis*: only, whereas the account of the Six Days of Creation is the definition by the Word of God of what is to manifest, Pan is the actual manifestation of that design and will of God.

One of the best contemporary expositions on Pan is by Francis Bacon, who explains the symbolism succinctly in his *Wisdom of the Ancients*:

> Pan, as the very word declares, represents the univer-
> sal frame of things, or Nature.[46] About his origin there
> are and can be but two opinions; for Nature is either
> the offspring of Mercury—that is of the Divine Word
> (an opinion which the Scriptures establish beyond
> question, and which was entertained by all the more
> divine philosophers); or else of the seeds of things
> mixed and confused together. For they who derive all
> things from a single principle, either take that principle
> to be God, or if they hold it to be a material principle,
> assert it to be though actually one yet potentially
> many; so that all difference of opinion on this point is
> reducible to one or other of these two heads,—the

world is sprung either from Mercury [Cupid], or from
all the suitors [Matter].....

For true it is that this Pan, whom we behold and contemplate and worship only too much, is sprung from
the Divine Word, through the medium of confused
matter (which is itself God's creature), and with the
help of sin and corruption entering in.[47]

Further on in his essay on Pan, Bacon describes the
office of Pan in a way that is most pertinent to *As You
Like It*:

Now the office of Pan can in no way be more lively set
forth and explained than by calling him god of
hunters. For every natural action, every motion and
process of nature, is nothing else than a hunt. For the
sciences and arts hunt after their works, human counsels
hunt after their ends, and all things in nature hunt
either after food, which is like hunting for prey, or
after their pleasures, which is like hunting for recre-
ation;—and that too by methods skilful and sagacious.

Also Pan is the god of country people in general;
because they live more according to nature; whereas
in courts and cities nature is corrupted by too much
culture....[48]

A Time Catechism

This Pan is synonymous with Saturn (the Greek Cronos),
the Lord of Time and son of Cupid.[49] Hence the allegorical
image of Pan is identical to that of Saturn or Time,
complete with his hour-glass and scythe. The evolutionary
aspect of Pan as the Time Lord is discussed in two jewels
of wisdom in the play: (1) the discourse by Jaques on the

seven ages of man (II, vii, 139-166), which has already
been discussed and on which the play itself is framed,
and (2) another kind of catechism, this time between
Rosalind and Orlando, in which Time is likened to a horse
(III, ii, 294-327):

> *Ros*. I pray you, what is't o'clock?
>
> *Orl*. You should ask me what time o' day; there's no
> clock in the forest.
>
> *Ros*. Then there's no true lover in the forest, else sighing
> every minute and groaning every hour would
> detect the lazy foot of Time, as well as a clock.
>
> *Orl*. And why not the swift foot of Time? Had not that
> been as proper?
>
> *Ros*. By no means sir. Time travels in divers paces with
> divers persons. I'll tell you who Time ambles withal,
> who Time trots withal, who Time gallops withal,
> and who he stands still withal.
>
> *Orl*. I prithee, who does he trot withal?
>
> *Ros*. Marry, he trots hard with a young maid, between
> the contract of her marriage and the day it is
> solemnized. If the interim be but a sennight,
> Time's pace is so hard that it seems the length of
> seven year.
>
> *Orl*. Who ambles Time withal?
>
> *Ros*. With a priest that lacks Latin, and a rich man that
> hath not the gout, for the one sleeps easily because
> he cannot study, and the other lives merrily
> because he feels no pain; the one lacking the burden
> of lean and wasteful learning; the other knowing
> no burden of heavy tedious penury. These Time
> ambles withal.
>
> *Orl*. Who doth he gallop withal?
>
> *Ros*. With a thief to the gallows; for though he go as

> softly as foot can fall, he thinks himself too soon
> there.
>
> *Orl.* Who stays it still withal?
>
> *Ros.* With lawyers in the vacation; for they sleep
> between term and term, and then they perceive not
> how Time moves.

There is more in this 'catechism' than meets the eye. Firstly, Pan is equated with the intelligence of nature, and all intelligence involves thinking, with its thoughts and dreams. Traditionally, thoughts are symbolised by horses: dark horses being nightmares, white horses being pure thoughts, winged white horses (*e.g.* Pegasus) being pure, lofty, inspired thoughts, and the winged unicorn signifying the pure, elevated, focused thought of the initiate. The rider of the horse is the ego, which through initiation can eventually become the true self—Cupid-Dionysus.

Secondly, the movement or speed of Time is a relative thing that is to do as much with consciousness as with physical reality. Time does indeed appear to go faster when the consciousness is intensely focused on something whose purpose it enjoys or, contrariwise, dreads; whilst it appears to go slowly to those who are bored or who are impatient for something to happen for which they long. As Rosalind says, 'Time travels in divers paces with divers persons'. The person or rider determines the pace of the horse.

Thirdly, the various speeds of the Time horse listed by Rosalind are expounded in a meaningful order, not haphazardly. This order relates to the life process, in which the expression of life moves from its first impulse to desire, then thought, then action, culminating with the final 'sleep' that comes at the end of the cycle.

Shakespeare denotes desire, the first expression of life, by means of the young maid who is in love and betrothed, and who is longing for her marriage day. For her, Time trots hard. The second expression is as thought, which requires comparisons, and this Shakespeare represents with the priest and rich man (*i.e.* the spiritual man and the material man), the one lacking 'the burden of lean and wasteful learning' and the other 'knowing no burden of heavy tedious penury'. For them, Time ambles. The third expression is as action, personified by the condemned thief who is on his way to meet his death on the gallows. For him, Time gallops. Death is indeed the end of the cycle, to which the action leads, and this death (or the state of being immediately after the moment of death) is often described as a sleep. The final expression of life is as this 'sleep', a rest after the cycle of work, which Shakespeare knowingly describes in terms of the exhausted lawyers who sleep in the vacation after each term.

Shakespeare has additionally arranged this exposition on Time so that the polarities of head (seat of thought) and abdomen (seat of action) are contrasted, with the medium of the chest (seat of desire) midway between— thought being represented as slow (ambling), action as fast (galloping), and desire as the midway balance of the other two (trotting). Moreover, it is in the passage concerning the betrothed young maid, which denotes the balance point (*i.e.* the chest and heart, seat of love), that the seven-fold law of life is mentioned by Rosalind in terms of the sennight (*i.e.* seven nights) or week which can seem the length of seven years: for it is love dwelling in the heart that is the supreme law, of which all other laws are aspects or subsidiaries. Once again, let us go to Francis Bacon's essay on 'Cupid, or the Atom' for a description of love that connects love with motion, as Shakespeare does, and as being the supreme or summary law of Creation:

This Love [Cupid] I understand to be the appetite or instinct [desire] of primal matter; or to speak more plainly, the natural motion of the atom; which is indeed the original and unique force that constitutes and fashions all things out of matter. Now this is entirely without parent; that is, without cause. For the cause is as it were parent of the effect; and of this virtue there can be no cause in nature (God always excepted): there being nothing before it, therefore no efficient; nor anything more original in nature, therefore neither kind nor form. Whatever it be, therefore, it is a thing positive and inexplicable. And even if it were possible to know the method and process of it, yet to know it by way of cause is not possible; it being, next to God, the cause of causes—itself without cause....with good reason therefore is it represented as an egg hatched by Night....

For the summary law of nature, that impulse of desire impressed by God upon the primary particles of matter which makes them come together, and which by repetition and multiplication produces all the variety of nature, is a thing which mortal thought may glance at, but can hardly take in. [50]

The Pan Tailpiece

Like Cupid-Dionysus, Pan is also represented pictorially in the 1st Shakespeare Folio. His image is to be found in an intricate tailpiece that is printed at the end of various plays. It first occurs at the end of the fourth play in the Folio, *Measure for Measure*, and then at the end of twenty-four further plays, including the last play in the Folio, *Cymbeline,* where it is printed on the very last page of the Folio. Its third occurrence is at the end of *As You Like It*.

The woodcut emblem depicts Pan sitting amidst what is known as the Frame of Nature—a typical Renaissance decorative feature in which nature is portrayed as the composite of an elaborate frame around which twines vegetable growth. The frame denotes the fixed aspect of nature—the physical laws and geometrical matrix of energy; whilst the vegetation represents the free-growing aspect. They are polarities to each other, neither existing without the other.

Pan is half-concealed within this frame, his face peering over a part of it that forms a kind of breastplate for him, heraldically imprinted with an eight-rayed star, or an eight-spoked elliptical wheel of fortune. As in other instances of this tailpiece, Pan has two pipes in his mouth which he is presumably playing, whilst his two arms are outstretched, one on each side, with each hand holding a cornucopia filled with fruits.

Immediately below Pan is drawn a female face set within a heart-shaped part of the frame. Pan's bride and

partner is Echo, and almost certainly this face is that of
Echo, whom Pan loves and by means of which he hears
and sees himself, thereby acquiring self-knowledge. She
is also known as Truth, which Pan, as Time, brings forth
from her hidden place in the heart. When Rosalind drops
her disguise and reveals herself at the end of the play,
truth is seen (V, iv, 117-118):

> *Duke Sen.* If there be truth in sight, you are my daughter.
> *Orl.* If there be truth in sight, you are my Rosalind.

Knowledge

Spiritual and Material Knowledge

Pan, as Saturn, is associated with knowledge. In Cabalistic
tradition, Saturn is equated with the Dark Angel of *Daath*
('Knowledge') and the Sabbath (*Sabbaoth*, 'Peace'), the
divine intelligence or mind that begins in a condition of
darkness (*i.e.* ignorance or sleep)[51] but which becomes
light when illumined by the light of love via Nature's
experience.

To see is not necessarily to know. To distinguish light
from dark is not necessarily to comprehend, although it is
a beginning of knowledge. True knowledge comes only
after experiencing the conditions of both light and dark,
and thus being able not only to distinguish the two but to
know what each means and is: and, furthermore, to *want*
the light. The acquisition of self-knowledge is said to be
the primary purpose of all creation and evolution, and
Pan, the divine intelligence embodied in Nature, is that
which acquires the knowledge. Indeed, when illumined,
Pan is said to be both the knower and that which is
known, which together constitutes total knowledge.

'HIDDEN TRUTH BROUGHT FORTH BY TIME'
Emblem from Titlepage of Francis Bacon's
New Atlantis, A Work unfinished (1626)

According to the tradition of Cabala, knowledge of God is
the goal of humanity:

> God created man in the mystery of Wisdom, and fash-
> ioned him with great art and breathed into him the breath
> of life, so that he might know and comprehend the mys-
> teries of Wisdom to apprehend the glory of his Lord.[52]

However, judging by human experience, it would seem that the desire to know all things has necessitated conditions of imperfection and illusion, with all grades of intelligence and types of knowledge, good and bad; which is why it is said that Saturn, as Satan, 'fell' from heaven and is in the process of being raised again, with the help of ministering angels, to become the crown jewel or holy grail of all Creation.

Knowledge is acquired by experience, and experiences are provided by each life cycle we undergo (*i.e.* impulse-desire-thought-action), large and small. In addition, however, we learn by means of comparisons. We know what light is when we can determine what light is not: likewise with good and bad, positive and negative, and so on. The ancient philosophers noted this as the polarity of life, of the universe, and defined it in various ways, chief of which were the polarities of light and dark, spirit and matter, active and passive, as initial phases; then wisdom and intelligence, compassion and judgment, desire and thought, as polarities of light; and friendship and strife, spirituality and materiality, good and evil, love and hate, as polarities of human experience. Except in terms of the very first and the last two, the perfect balance of these is harmony, from which arises beauty and then joy. With light and darkness, however, darkness is simply a lack of light: it is 'swallowed up' by light and ceases to exist. With good and evil, love and hate, evil and hate are distortions of truth as well as arising through a lack of goodness and love: therefore, when love and goodness become strong, evil and hate will ultimately vanish.

In the Hermetic and Cabalistic tradition, each polarity is signified by a pillar (*e.g.* the twin pillars of a temple entrance) and the characteristics of each polarity is represented by the planetary spirits. For instance, Jupiter and

Venus denote compassion and affection respectively, on the right-hand pillar of wisdom, whilst Mars and Mercury stand for judgment and reason, on the left-hand pillar of intelligence. These pillars were also known to the Orphic philosophers as friendship and strife, for friendship's love is affectionate and compassionate, whilst the mind strives in its thinking to organise, test, command and know. From the primordial point of view, the right-hand pillar is associated with spirit and light, whilst the left-hand pillar is associated with matter and the dark: for this is the condition before spirit enters matter and gives it life and form, and before light illuminates the darkness, giving it understanding and knowledge.

The knowledge of these polarities, in their primal sense, can be summed up as spiritual knowledge and material knowledge. These Shakespeare has personified in the characters of the two Dukes—the underlying subject matter of *As You Like It.*

The Two Dukes

The deposed Duke (Duke Senior) is characterised as having a loving and contemplative nature, who studies nature and listens to people like Jaques intently, desiring to know all he can by such means. He is described as a good man, jovial in spirit, friendly to others, and demonstrates compassion and affection. In this, he clearly possesses spiritual knowledge, which is equated with love and wisdom; and, as knowledge is power, he has spiritual power as the magician who teaches his daughter and as the Robin Hood who leads his merry men. However, like Prospero in *The Tempest,* he has lost control of his dukedom to his younger brother.

Duke Frederick, on the other hand, is someone who might be described as both worldly-wise and sinister. His knowledge is of worldly things, how to obtain them and how to hold on to them. He is martial in spirit, strives against people and desires worldly possessions and power, which he has acquired and continues to acquire by force or cunning. Worldly knowledge and power in itself is not a bad thing by any means: it is something which Duke Senior was probably sadly lacking. However, when coupled with a desire that is selfish and possessive, it becomes a serious problem.

At the culmination of the play, Duke Frederick gives up all his worldly wealth and desires, and chooses instead to follow a religious calling or spiritual life: '[Duke Frederick,] meeting with an old religious man, after some question with him, was converted both from his enterprise and from the world…' (v, iv, 159-161). The two Jaques' later confirm that Duke Frederick has 'put on a religious life' (v, iv, 179-182). Moving from a position of material knowledge and power, Duke Frederick now desires spiritual knowledge, to be gained by him through religious experience.

Duke Senior, his dukedom returned to him, as a result prepares to return to court, to take up the governance of his land and people. Having acquired knowledge of life's laws from his experience in the forest, and at the same time being a good or spiritual man, he is now better fitted for his responsible task as head of state.

Knowledge of God's Word & God's Works

Spiritual knowledge and material knowledge can also be understood in terms of what Francis Bacon calls the Book of God's Word and Book of God's Works, in both of which, he urges, we should be well read. This is ancient wisdom and practice. The Book of God's Word is Wisdom, inspired direct into our hearts or revealed to us through the prophets and holy scriptures. The Book of God's Works is Nature, the Cosmos. The divine studies the Book of God's Word: the philosopher learns through a study of nature, metaphysical as well as physical. The one is the path of the mystic and theologist, the other that of the scientist and cosmologist. Both paths are needed for any complete knowledge: for personal guidance and break-throughs in science are accomplished by means of inspiration and intuition, whilst mystical revelation and wisdom teaching require scientific verification, as far as is possible, to ensure that they are valid and not man-made fancy or illusion. These two aspects of knowledge are manifestations of how life was brought into being in the first place: for Pan, the universe, was created by means of both the Divine Word and Matter. Both are partners in the scheme of life.

In *As You Like It,* the philosopher aspect is carefully emphasised in the person of the banished Duke, who studies nature avidly and yet is a mystic searching to know himself (II, i, 1-17):

> *Duke Sen.* Now my co-mates and brothers in exile,
> Hath not old custom made this life more sweet
> Than that of painted pomp? Are not these woods
> More free from peril than the envious court?
> Here feel we not the penalty of Adam,
> The seasons' difference, as the icy fang
> And churlish chiding of the winter's wind,
> Which when it bites and blows upon my body
> Even till I shrink with cold, I smile, and say
> 'This is no flattery. These are counsellors

> That feelingly persuade me what I am'.
> Sweet are the uses of such adversity,
> Which like the toad, ugly and venomous,
> Wears yet a precious jewel in his head;
> And this our life, exempt from public haunt,
> Finds tongues in trees, books in running brooks,
> Sermons in stones, and good in everything.

'Know thyself!' was the enjoiner to every pupil and initiate who entered the great temple of Apollo at Delphi. As Cicero remarked: '[Philosophy] has taught us not only all other things but also something that is very difficult; that we should know ourselves: the force of that precept is so great, the thought behind it so great, that it should not be attributed to any man but to the Delphic god.'[53]

The Two Jaques

The Duke is not the only one who is deliberately seeking for knowledge in the play. Orlando, Rosalind and Celia can be said to have some good knowledge and gain more as the play progresses, but it is Jaques who represents the faculty of the mind in its search for truth more than any other character. Saturn, or Pan, is Intelligence and the Knowledge which that intelligence gathers. Saturn is also known as the ruler of the melancholy humour—the pre-eminent humour of Jaques. This does not necessarily mean depression, and Jaques nowhere displays a depressive nature. He can be jovial, with song, and enjoys people's company: but he observes, he thinks, he draws out morals from what he sees, and he envies Touchstone, the court jester, for his professional capacity to heal the world by means of his wit. Melancholy is that humour which is associated with curiosity and deep thought, and is the beginning of knowledge, having the capacity to dig deep into the psychological darkness. Light is born in darkness, and Saturn's melancholy is just such a darkness.

However, there are two characters by the name of Jaques—the melancholic courtier Jaques and Jaques de Boys, middle brother to Oliver and Orlando. These two personify the two major ways of learning: (1) learning by studying nature and one's experiences in nature, which includes both human and divine nature, and (2) learning by means of academic study.

8. The City and the Forest

The Significance of Place

The settings which Shakespeare uses for his plays are an integral part of the stories, and likewise they are integral to the wisdom and philosophy in each play. Certain things happen in certain places and not others, and for this reason places themselves have come to symbolise certain things in human life. Just as the abdomen in the human body is the place for the assimilation of food and drink, the procreative functions of sex, *etc.*, so the inn or market place, or whorehouse, are representative of this in drama as well as in real life. Likewise with the head—the place for thinking, organising, law-making, *etc.*—the law court, parliament or some place of administration is used in drama to highlight those activities. For the heart or chest functions, places midway between inn and court are often used, or secret places for lovers, or churches and temples, or the royal court and palace. (Alternatively, the palace is representative of the crown, 'crowning' the head.) In other words, there is a whole symbolic language concerning places—places having roles like people.[54] The Classical and Renaissance stage was usually arranged so that all the required places could be identifiable on stage, all at the same time if necessary, according to where they were positioned.

The Wisdom of Shakespeare in *As You Like It*

In Mystery plays, such as Shakespeare's Comedies, the places also represent different levels or worlds of existence, such as the heavens, world and underworld of Greek myth. That is to say, besides the more literal interpretation of the play and its setting that can be made, there is another level of interpretation—or several other levels. For instance, in *As You Like It* there are two main places used in the story—the city and the forest . The city, containing the ducal palace and the house and garden of the de Boys brothers, is the home of the Duke, the princesses, courtiers, lords, gentlemen and townsfolk. The forest, on the other hand, is the environment of the country folk—the peasants, farmers and outlaws. The action moves from the city to focus almost entirely upon the forest, which is the place where the transformations and marriages take place. At the end of the play we are informed that there will be a return to the city, in triumph and joy.

There is a similarity in this arrangement with many other Shakespeare plays, *The Tempest* being perhaps the closest analogy. *The Winter's Tale* is another. Looked at in simple terms, the city with its royal court and gentlemen's houses is a place where man-made laws and culture reign, whilst the countryside and forest, like Prospero's island, is nature's domain, where human culture has only slight effect and nature's laws are dominant. It can therefore be understood that the former represents humanity and the latter, nature.

What appears to have already occurred at the start of the story of *As You Like It* is that the court and city have become corrupted by too much culture (see 'Pan', Chapter 7), the result being that the rightful rulership has been usurped and banished, along with many of the good lords. Man-made laws have obscured the spiritual and natural laws of the universe, instead of reflecting them, and the rule of law in the metropolis has become one not of justice but of tyranny. Shakespeare postulates in his play that this situation is corrected only by a return to nature where there is less artificial culture and less corruption, and where the spiritual laws that can transmute the situation to something better are able to operate far more freely: only, at the same time Shakespeare is not saying that man should remain for ever in retreat in nature, but should learn what he needs and then return to society to serve it responsibly.

The situation implies that an imbalance has occurred between man and nature which has to be corrected, and this we can see being done in the person of the banished Duke, who takes great pains to study and learn from nature those things that he did not know before. Once changed for the better, the lords, ladies, gentlemen and Duke can return to their homes in the city and institute a better state of affairs, with a cleansed and revitalised culture that reflects better the universal laws.

There are two distinct ways in which this situation and the two respective places can be analysed in terms of the Neoplatonic-Cabalistic philosophy. For instance, translated into more cosmological terms the city would appear to signify the realm of the human psyche, whilst the forest represents the natural or physical world into which the human soul needs, at times, to incarnate, and where spirit and soul, like gold and silver, are forged together as one in Vulcan's workshop. Or else the two places, forest and city, can be understood to represent the right-hand and left-hand 'pillars' respectively of life, which need to be perfectly balanced and blended by the human soul.

The Two Pillars

In Neoplatonic tradition, the globe of the earth, representing nature, is related to the right-hand 'solar' pillar of wisdom, mercy and emotion, whilst the globe of the mind, representing the psyche, is related to the left-hand 'lunar' pillar of intelligence, judgment and thought. One reason for this is to imply that the spiritual laws of the universe, associated with wisdom, are manifested directly in nature, whilst in the human psyche they are reflected as mirror images. The human psyche is itself an 'image' of the Word or Wisdom of God in the divine mind, but this image can be obscured or even impaired by human free-will. It is left to the human soul to choose to mirror the spiritual truths or not, and we are allowed to make mistakes: although we are always called to account eventually and have to correct or pay for those mistakes. Through mistakes and imperfections it would seem that we can learn what perfection is and how to become more perfect as human souls, although there are probably other more congenial ways of learning as well. All the while, however, the human spirit is the divine wisdom incarnate in our hearts and sometimes imprisoned there, waiting to be released so that it can guide and illuminate the soul.

The key to human evolution is to be able to develop both heart and mind, to allow the spirit to shine ever brighter and the mind (the psyche) to reflect and be illuminated by that light with as much clarity and accuracy as possible. When matters become imbalanced, weaknesses and distortions occur that allow evil to take control. Fortunately for us, however, love ultimately corrects the imbalance, for love is the supreme power.

In *As You Like It* we can see the imbalance and distortion of truth, which exists at the beginning of the play, being

TITLEPAGE TO THE 1640 EDITION OF FRANCIS BACON'S
OF THE ADVANCEMENT AND PROFICIENCE OF LEARNING,
—the English translation by Gilbert Wats of Francis Bacon's
De Dignitate et Augmentis Scientiarum 1623.

rebalanced and corrected. All the city characters are, for one reason or another, made to leave the human metropolis and either visit or live in the natural environment, learning direct from nature. Once the balance has been achieved, and the corruption purged, the characters are able (or allowed) to return again to their human realm.

Heaven and Earth

When looked at from the more cosmological point of view, the story of *As You Like It* is a variation on the Greek Mystery theme of Persephone, who is seduced or abducted forcibly from her world and taken into the underworld by Hades. The underworld in Greek myth signifies the natural, physical world or universe, whilst Persephone and her world personifies the human psyche, the personal soul. Persephone's story is an allegory of the incarnation of the human soul into the material, corporeal world where, after experience in that underworld, she is able to be rescued by Hermes and return to her true home, pregnant with a child of light. When this child (Dionysus) is born, Persephone dies and the child takes her place. In other words, the old situation, which was one of weakness and mistakes, is completely changed—dies, in fact—and goodness, joy and light take its place. The soul has thereby evolved, which is said to be the purpose of all incarnation.

Another allegory which tells the same story is that of Adam and Eve, who represent the male-female soul in its hermaphroditical infancy. According to Cabalistic teaching, their Garden of Eden existed on the soul level, the 'World of Formation' or realm of the psyche. When they were cast out of the Edenic paradise for disobeying God's command, they entered the corporeal and mortal world of nature. Ultimately, through the incarnatory and evolutionary process, the first Adam will become the second Adam or Christ, and the first Eve will become the Virgin Mary or mother of that Christ, the child of light. Both will be taken up to heaven, and heaven will be changed as a result. This is the story and goal of each human soul, as already demonstrated for us, even though it might take many incarnatory efforts to reach the height of perfection.

The City

I use the term 'city' in a metaphorical sense, as there is no description in the play of an actual city, but only of a ducal palace with its court and gardens, a public space in front of the palace where gentlemen and commoners alike can gather and where the wrestling match takes place, and the house and garden of the De Boys family. This could be a description of anything from a bustling metropolis to a small medieval town that is associated with the palace-fortress of a duke, in which or near which are situated the houses of gentlemen and courtiers. The word 'city' is derived from the Latin *civitas*, a self-governing town or state in which live citizens. It is a place where the law of man regulates and rules society, although in *As You Like It* some at least of those laws are perverted or circumscribed because of the reign of the tyrant, Duke Frederick, who does what he pleases.

For the Ardennes setting of *As You Like It*, Shakespeare probably had in mind a typical French or Belgium ducal capital, with access to extensive forests and pastureland used by the aristocracy for hunting and picnics. Or he may even have been thinking of the Dukes of Burgundy, the 'Great Dukes of the West', of whom

Philip the Good (who reigned 1419-1467) held a court that surpassed that of any contemporary sovereign. The Grand Dukes were recognised as sovereign princes and their domains included the Netherlands, Ardennes and Luxembourg, as well as their more southerly lands in France. This latter view tends to be supported by the fact that Shakespeare keeps the princesses of Lodge's poem whilst transforming Lodge's two kings into dukes.

Present in Shakespeare's *As You Like It* metropolis is the house of the De Boys family and the palace of the Duke, where resides the court. The De Boys house includes an orchard in its garden, which, with the inclusion of Adam in it at the very beginning of the play, is a clear indication that the city signifies the Eden of the psychological world. Both house and palace are representative of two of the many 'mansions' in heaven which Jesus once spoke about.[55]

According to the biblical account in *Genesis*, in the centre of Eden lies the orchard containing both the tree of knowledge of good and evil and the tree of life.[56] Both are denied to the human soul at the beginning, but Adam and Eve precipitate the incarnational and evolutionary path that will lead to their earning and gaining their ultimate inheritance (*i.e.* to be the image or likeness of God). This involves them eating the apple of knowledge and being cast out of Eden as a result. They have to fall to the earth realm where in sorrow Eve brings forth children ('in sorrow thou shalt bring forth children, and thy desire shall be to thy husband…'[57]), and Adam has to 'till the ground'[58] as its gardener.[58] This 'penalty of Adam' is referred to by Duke Senior in his first speech (II, i, 5).

The work which Adam is obliged to carry out is an echo of the soul's purpose in the Edenic Paradise: for the decree given to mankind (male and female) was to be a gardener in Eden, 'to dress it and to keep it',[59] having 'dominion over' (*i.e.* looking after) what has been created, as well as to be fruitful and multiply, and to 'behold' (*i.e.* see, understand and know).[60]

From this biblical analogy, it is clear that the De Boys orchard is representative of the orchard at the heart of Eden and that Orlando is the one who is being tempted to seek better things. He is not content with the decree of his elder brother, which he considers unjust and which keeps him 'rustically at home'. Like Adam in the Garden of Eden, Orlando realises he is 'naked' and precipitates his own exile. Challenging both his brother and, indirectly, Duke Frederick, he is forced to flee his home for the forest, in fear of his life. He doesn't want to leave his home which, except for the condition in which his brother keeps him, he loves; therefore, he flees the city in sorrow.

Rosalind does likewise, but the home from which she is banished is the palace. She precipitates her banishment by showing love and support for Orlando in the face of Duke Frederick's openly declared antagonism towards the young gentleman. Yearning to be the wife of Orlando and the mother of his child, she also departs the city in sorrow.

However, the Eden that is symbolised by the De Bois house and ducal palace is not the perfect Eden, for it contains imperfection and people who are far from innocent. Rather, it is the imperfect Eden known in Cabala as the Lower Eden, a 'shadow' of the pure Upper Eden. The task of the human soul is to gradually perfect this Lower Eden and raise it to merge with the seven heavens of the Upper Eden. To do this, the soul needs to incarnate into the natural world, where the necessary lessons, challenges and purifications can take place.

The Forest

The Ardennes

The Forest of Arden refers to the Ardennes bordering Belgium and Luxembourg, and extending west-east from France to the Rhineland. One small western part lies in France, north-east of Reims. The Ardennes consist of the eroded base of a mountain chain that was once as high as the Alps, forming a romantic landscape of flat-topped hills, gorges and wider valleys, mostly covered with woods that are among the most beautiful in Europe, but with pastoral land picturesquely disposed. The extensive woods comprise what remains of the Forest of Ardenne, once the greatest in Gaul, named by the Romans as the *Arduenna Sylva*, from the Celtic word *ardu*, 'dark, obscure'—hence the meaning 'dark forest'. Another associated derivation of the word is from *ar-Denn* or *ar-Tann*, Breton for 'the oaks' or 'among the oaks'.[61]

Besides the plentiful oaks, the forest was once well stocked with wild game—red and roe deer, wild boar, *etc.*. The lioness, though, is an invention of Shakespeare, although there is no doubt that this 'dark oak forest' could be frightening and dangerous enough in days of few roads and no maps, where armed robbers could surprise you, miles upon miles of dark, lonely woods and dense thickets could confound you, poisonous snakes could bite you and ferocious boar could maim or kill you. It is not surprising that Rosalind arms herself with a cutlass and a boar-spear (I, iii, 113-114). However, the forest was also a place where it was possible to survive, and survive reasonably well. Furthermore, because there used to be a separate forest law governing the lives of those dwelling in forests, forest dwellers were outside the protection (and demands) of the common and civil laws operating elsewhere. For these reasons it was a good place for rogues and exiles to hide in and make their home, as outlaws, and for poor country folk to live in relative peace.

Arcadia and the Golden Age

In Shakespeare's time the Ardennes were famous for their romantic quality and provided the ideal setting for an Arcadia, the name of the Greek country (in the Peloponnese) that is reputed to have enjoyed a golden age. The original golden age was that of Adam and Eve in the Garden of Eden before their fall from grace. The name *Arden* reminds us of this Eden, a veritable paradise. Arcadia was an alternative name, harking back to the time of Atlantis when the world, or a large part of it, enjoyed a golden age under the guidance of Enoch, the great teacher and king of Atlantis.

The expectancy of a new golden age was very real to the Elizabethans, who associated their 'Virgin Queen', Elizabeth, with the rulership of such an age. Virgil had prophesied the return of a golden age in his *Aeneid*, mentioning that it would be introduced by the reign of the Virgin Astraea, or Justice, who would give birth to a child that would rule a world reconciled with itself and at peace. Elizabeth was symbolically associated with this Virgin, proclaimed as such by the poets and dressed up to play the part.[62]

Besides the Virgin Queen, Saturn is reputed to rule over the golden age. In fact, the two can be equated (like the opposite sides of the same coin), accounting for Rosalind's remark: 'Well, Time is the old Justice that examines all such offenders, and let Time try' (IV, i, 189-190).

Moreover, the god of Arcadia is reputed to be the great god Pan. When it is realised that Pan and Saturn are identical, and that Saturn-Pan is the god (or goddess) of Peace, this makes sense. The emblem on the title page of Lodge's *Rosalynde* refers to such a golden age, its motto declaring: 'By wisdom, peace; by peace, plenty'. The wand of Mercury, the clasped hands of friendship and the over-flowing cornucopia illustrate these three ingredients of a golden age, by means of which it is attained. Other Elizabethan poets used the same imagery, Edmund Spenser and Sir Philip Sydney being the most famous.

The Arcadians were shepherds, goatherds, cattle-herders and hunters in their once beautiful and idyllic country. They considered themselves to be the most ancient people in Greece, and more ancient than the moon. They were passionately fond of music, poetry and pastoral song, as also of learning, for all of which they became famous. They were also hunters and warriors, protecting their country. For this reason Apollo and

Artemis were, together with Pan, also known as the chief divinities of Arcadia—Apollo being a god of music and learning, and Artemis being a goddess of the hunt. Interestingly, acorns are said to have formed a large part of the Arcadians' diet, as the country was once well planted with oak trees.[63]

The Arcadian image of the learned shepherd-warrior became the Elizabethan courtier's ideal. Spenser portrayed this dual ideal separately in his *Shepherd's Calendar* and his *Faerie Queene*, the former dealing with the shepherd and latter with the warrior or knight of the Round Table. In *As You Like It,* Shakespeare also portrays each aspect separately, with Rosalind and Celia becoming involved with shepherds and shepherdesses, and becoming shepherdesses themselves in the pastureland, whilst the good Duke and his 'merry men', plus Orlando and Oliver, live as hunters in the oak forest. When Orlando and Rosalind, and Celia and Oliver, marry, they in effect unite the two aspects of the Arcadian ideal.

King Arthur and the Round Table

Pan, or Saturn, the god of Arcadia, is the Greek god Cronos, the Lord of Time. In Celtic myth the great solar king, Arthur, bears a resemblance to Cronos, only he is greater than Pan. Arthur is the Sun, the spiritual Light. His throne is the 13th seat of the zodiacal Round Table, located at the centre of the Zodiac (*i.e.* the Occult Pole); although he has another seat in the zodiacal circle itself, when represented by the sun that moves around the ecliptic in the company of the planets. The Zodiac with its twelve signs and 'creatures'[64] is his Round Table of knights and ladies. They number twenty-four, with one knight and lady equated with each sign of the Zodiac.

The King himself has his Queen, his 'Holy Grail' whom he has to protect as Guardian of the Grail. She is the 'Faerie Queene' of Spenser's tale, who outwardly was personified by the red-haired Tudor Queen Elizabeth, whose ancestry was Welsh (*i.e.* Celtic). The family home of the Tudors used to lie on Anglesey, the principal sacred island of the British Druids. Beginning with Elizabeth's grandfather, Henry VII, a strong revival of the Arthurian myth was instituted in Merry England. England's premier Order of the Garter, originally known as the Order of St. George and the Round Table, acted out the myths ceremonially, and Garter processions and feasts became an important part of Tudor England—as also did the tournaments, at which courtier-knights tilted at each other, demonstrating their courage and skill before their Faerie Queen. In Elizabeth's reign, these tournaments were enlarged to become great public spectacles of drama, art, learning and knightly prowess—entertainments on a grandiose scale for her courtiers and subjects that were organised each year as a celebration of the Queen's Accession Day (November 17th).

Robin Hood and his Merry Men

The Arthurian story, with its cosmological significance, is found in many forms and in many countries. France's famous equivalent was that of Charles the Great (Charlemagne) and the Twelve Worthies of France, mentioned in Lodge's *Rosalynde* and from which are derived the names of Orlando, Rowland and Oliver in *As You Like It*. Another English personification of the myth is to be found in the story of Robin Hood and his Merry Men. Robin Hood is an Arthurian figure, but pictured as a humble king-saviour of the common people rather than as an aristocratic king-warrior of nations. Like Arthur, Robin has both an archetypal as well as historical reality, the various historical persons equated with the god being folk heroes whom the people have identified with the myth.

For instance, Robin Hood is reputed to be an expert archer, like Cupid whom he represents. As in Ancient Egyptian symbolism, his bow and arrows signify the heart and the radiant love-light of the heart respectively. His hood denotes wisdom as well as concealment, like the helmet of Pallas Athena, whilst his name 'Robin' is linked with the red-breasted bird of that name. The red breast was perceived as representing love poured out for others in self-sacrifice, as with the iconographic pelican which pierces its breast to feed its young. In a more ferocious time the sun-heroes were actually sacrificed by their community at the end of each year. In later centuries the robin was taken as a substitute for the sun-hero or king, and the bird used to be slaughtered annually instead, using a bow and arrows. The song, 'Who killed Cock Robin?' is a reminder of this old custom.

The historical Robin Hood, who lived at the time of King Richard I (the Lion-Heart), lived in Sherwood Forest, which tradition ascribes to the forest bordering on Nottingham. Sherwood Forest was far greater then than it is today, and the real 'dark forest' lay much further north, the road through it leading southwards from York to Nottingham being very dangerous to travel on due to outlaws and other dangers.

According to Gypsy lore, this area where the historical Robin Hood made his home with his merry men is associated with the zodiacal sign of Leo. This key sign and area is part of a great landscape Zodiac or 'Round Table' laid out geomantically and mythologically across Britain, as a reflection of the celestial pattern, which the Gypsies used to make a circuit of during the course of each year. Leo, the Lion, which is ruled by the Sun according to astrological lore, is the sign of the Sun-King; therefore it is entirely appropriate and in keeping with folk tradition for the outlawed sun-hero to have his 'royal' seat there. The name of the forest, *Sherwood*, is an old name meaning 'Shining Wood' or 'Forest of Light' (from *sheer* or *shere*, meaning 'bright', 'shining'), which matches its solar position in the British Zodiac. Interestingly, the historical 12th-century Robin Hood originally came from a family home in a Warwickshire village called Loxley, where he was born and bred, which lies just south of Warwick and not far from Stratford-upon-Avon. Thus the folk hero actually originated from the Warwickshire Forest of Arden.

Robin Hood's merry men traditionally number twelve and, although they doubtless had a sense of humour, their name is actually derived from Mary, the Virgin and Bride of the Christ, the Sun-King. They are dedicated to her as guardians and servants. Mary is the Holy Grail, the 'Pure Vessel' of Catholic tradition that can conceive and bear the Christ Child of light. She corresponds to the Celtic Bridget or Bride, the flame-haired virgin goddess whom the red-haired Queen Elizabeth personified so well. She is vitally important to the history of Britain, as she is the country's primary goddess. Britain is named after her (*i.e.* as Britannia or *Brit-Anna*, 'the Chosen of Anna', Mary being Anna's child or 'chosen one'), and the land is still known in Roman Catholic tradition as 'the Dowry of the Virgin Mary'. England carries on that tradition in its appellation as Merry England.

The twelve Mary men are the English folk equivalent of Christ's twelve apostles, or Arthur's twelve knights. They wear Lincoln green because green is the Celtic colour of the virgin goddess, symbolic of harmony, purity and everlasting life, and because the town of Lincoln is in the area of the British Zodiac corresponding to the zodiacal sign of Virgo, the Virgin.

In *As You Like It,* the good Duke is likened to Robin Hood. His followers, who have given up land and titles and wealth to be with him as outlaws in the forest, are his 'merry men' (I, i, 114-119):

> *Charles.* They say he is already in the Forest of Arden, and a many merry men with him; and there they live like the old Robin Hood of England. They say many young gentlemen flock to him every day, and fleet the time carelessly as they did in the golden world.

The Cryptic Greek Invocation

This act of friendship and devotion is the subject of a parody by Jaques, when he completes Amiens' Arcadian song about the young gentlemen who have left all to live in the forest with their Duke (Act II, scene 5):

> *Amiens:*
>
> Under the greenwood tree,
> Who loves to lie with me,
> And turn his merry note
> Unto the sweet bird's throat,
> Come hither, come hither, come hither.
> Here shall he see
> No enemy,
> But winter and rough weather.

Who doth ambition shun,
    And loves to live i' th' sun,
Seeking the food he eats,
    And pleas'd with what he gets,
Come hither, come hither, come hither.
    Here shall he see
    No enemy,
But winter and rough weather.

Jaques:
If it do come to pass
    That any man turn ass,
Leaving his wealth and ease,
    A stubborn will to please,
Ducdame, ducdame, ducdame,
    Here shall he see
    Gross fools as he,
And if he will come to me.

Amiens does not immediately understand all that Jaques says, although he obviously recognises the general meaning, whose context follows his own. Amiens asks what Jaques means by 'ducdame', which is Jaques' substitute for Amien's 'Come hither':

Amiens. What's that 'ducdame'?

Jaques. 'Tis a Greek invocation, to call fools into a circle.

Jaques doesn't give much away, but his words actually have deep meaning and show that he perceives very clearly what is going on. Although he tells Amiens that it is a Greek invocation, he is actually using French words which Amiens, as a French nobleman, must have recognised, but without understanding. Jaques' description of the invocation being Greek is almost certainly because the cryptic sing-song cant of beggars was known as 'Pedlar's Greek'. In other words, Jaques is pointing out in his biting satire that the lords who have left their lands and wealth to join the Duke are 'gross fools' who have made themselves beggars, and that the invocation that has been the cause of them leaving all worldly things is 'ducdame'.

This seemingly strange word is comprised of two French words, *duc* meaning 'duke' and *dame* meaning 'lady': hence, as Amiens must have first thought, Jaques is apparently referring to the Duke and his lady. However, the Duke's wife, Rosalind's mother, is never mentioned in the play and can only be presumed long since deceased. The Duke's company in the forest is an all male one. However, as an allegory, if the Duke is Robin Hood, an Arthurian figure, then his lady is none other than Lady Marion (*i.e.* Mary) or Queen Guinevere ('the White Lady')—the Virgin Goddess. Their combined names, indicating their love union, is indeed the call sign to all Mary Men and Knights of the Round Table to come into (*i.e.* form) a circle.

There is further meaning to be discovered if the invocation is taken as *duc d'ame*, so as to rhyme with 'come to me' of the final line, as Amiens did in his two verses. The word *ame* means 'soul' and *ami* means 'friend', both being associated with the word *amour*, 'love'. In other words, the cause of the gentlemen flocking to the Duke and joining his magic circle or Round Table is the Duke's own soul or friendship. They come to him out of love, in friendship, for that is what he is to them. His love and friendship calls them, shining brightly from the heart of his sun-self, his Arthurian Robin Hood nature. It is the Duke's soul and the soul of each of us that is the 'lady', the holy grail that shines with light when filled with love.

The wittiness of Jaques' satire is completed by the similarity of *ducdame* to the Welsh (Cymric) *Dewch da mi*, meaning 'come to me' (*i.e.* 'come hither'),[65] which presumably Shakespeare must have learnt, just as he knew so much about other Celtic matters. It is too much of a coincidence for it to have been by chance.

The Hidden Cave

The magic circle of the Round Table is equated with the ecliptic or celestial path that the sun appears to take through the twelve signs of the Zodiac each year. Its celestial centre is the Occult Pole, the axial centre of the ecliptic. In terrestrial terms, wherein the earth reflects the heavens according to the Hermetic maxim ('As above, so below, *etc.*.')[66], this occult or hidden centre corresponds to Duke Senior's cave. Like Robin Hood, the good Duke has a secret home in the forest, which he describes as a cave (II, vii, 200). Because he is representative of the Sun-King, lord of the zodiacal circle of time, who himself is the centre of his own magic circle of light, his concealed lair is the hidden centre of his Round Table, the Zodiac into which he calls his friends.

The symbolism of the cave for such a secret (and sacred) place is universal. It signifies a heart centre, the spiritual womb of light. In the Christian story, for instance, Jesus was born in a cave surrounded by animals (*i.e.* creatures of the Zodiac). In Hindu myth, Shiva is reputed to be born in a cave in the side of his sacred mountain, Kailash. In Arthurian myth, King Arthur has a cave in the Mount of Avalon to which he is conveyed by boat when he is mortally wounded. There he is said to sleep with his knights until a hero wakes him up at a time when the country is in danger and his help is needed.

Merlin, Arthur's teacher and predecessor, likewise retires to a cave in a crystal mountain (or island) when he has completed his work. There he waits and watches in the company of eleven companions and nine ranks of bards, who attend him and who guard the Thirteen Treasures of Britain and Merlin's books of wisdom. Merlin waits until such time as a certain fair youth will ring the bell at the cave entrance, causing the door to open and allowing the youth to enter, read the books of wisdom and be instructed by the great sage.

The Merlin myth was surely in Shakespeare's mind when he concluded the play with Jaques' reply to the Duke's request (V, iv, 193-195):

> *Duke Sen.* Stay, Jaques, stay.
> *Jaques.* To see no pastime, I. What you would have
>   I'll stay to know at your abandon'd cave.

Merlin is a title associated with the Sun-god that denotes his wisdom. It is equivalent in meaning to Logos, or Hermes, or Thoth, or Mercury, the Word. Sometimes it was given to leaders—sun-kings—of great note: for a true *ard-rig* (high king) of Ancient Britain was expected to be both a heroic warrior-prince, capable of defending his people and the truth, and an arch-druid. The historical 5th-century Merlin, for instance, is now generally acknowledged to have been Aurelius Ambrosius ('Prince of the Sanctuary'), Arthur's uncle and the high king of Britain prior to the reign of Arthur, son of Uther Pendragon.

Probably the most famous cave in Shakespeare's plays is Prospero's in *The Tempest*. There Shakespeare makes it clear that it is, like Merlin's cave, the magician's secret retreat and home. However, there is another cave in another play which relates directly to Merlin and

British myth, and that is Belarius' cave in *Cymbeline*—
Belarius, like Merlin, raising the King's two sons away
from court and in the wildness of nature.

The Cottage & Sheep-cote

If the Duke's cave in the forest is one heart centre, then
there is another for the ladies, the two princesses, who
are the centre of their own universe. In this,
Shakespeare deals with another great truth under the
veil of entertaining drama.

Helped by Corin, Rosalind and Celia buy the shepherd's
cottage which Silvius had been thinking of purchasing.
Together with the cottage, as part of the purchase, they
take possession of the flock of sheep, the pastureland
and the sheepcote. When Oliver comes looking for the
princesses, as Orlando's messenger, he describes the
place he is looking for as being on the edge of the
forest and where there is a sheepcote surrounded with
olive trees. Celia completes the description for him (IV,
iii, 75-82):

> *Oliver*. Good morrow, fair ones. Pray you, if you know,
>> Where in the purlieus of this forest stands
>> A sheep-cote fenc'd about with olive-trees?
> *Celia*. West of this place, down in the neighbour
>> bottom.
>> The rank of osiers by the murmuring stream
>> Left on your right hand, brings you to the place.
>> But at this hour the house doth keep itself,
>> There's none within.

The description of the princesses' home is that of a
place of peace, symbolised by the sheepcote (sheepfold).
In biblical terminology, sheep and shepherds and

pastures and sheepcotes have traditionally been associated with peace and peaceful activities. Jesus referred to the mystery associated with this when he described himself as the good Shepherd and his disciples as his sheep: 'I am the good Shepherd: the good Shepherd giveth his life for his sheep.'[67] He also described himself as the door of the sheepfold: 'I am the door: by me, if any man enter in, he shall be saved, and shall go in and out, and find pasture'.[68]

The symbolism and description, besides being an allegory of the human soul, has also a symbolic place that is represented in the stars like all other great myths. The constellation concerned with this is *Ursa Minor*, 'the Little Bear'. This is not its original name. Its earlier Hebraic name was *Dōhver*, meaning 'a fold of animals', particularly a sheepfold. Its related word, *Dōhveh*, means 'rest' or 'security'. But a possible confusion set in during translation to other languages, by mistaking the name for the Hebrew word *Dōhv*, which means 'a bear'. The Arabians then called the constellation *Al Dubb al Asghar*, 'the Lesser Bear'. The Phoenicians called it *Doube* or *Dōbher*, but this meant to them 'the Speaking or Guiding One'.[69]

Ursa Minor's seven stars contain one in particular, named (in Arabic) *Al Ruccaba*, 'the turned upon', which today is our *Polaris* or North Pole Star. Around this star the heavens appear to rotate as the Earth spins on its axis. Besides spinning, however, the Earth wobbles on its axis, meaning that the Earth's Celestial North Pole (*i.e.* the world's axis 'projected' into the sky and reflected there on the imaginary celestial 'dome') makes an imaginary circle in the sky about the Occult North Pole, which would be our permanent Celestial North Pole if the Earth did not wobble. It takes approximately 26,000 years to complete this circle, and so once every 26,000 years the world's Celestial North Pole coincides with *Al Ruccaba*.

As far as it appears to anyone on Earth at any time, it is the Celestial North Pole and its nearest star that is for us the central hub of the universe, with all the constellations spinning around it every day in a great wheel of motion. At this present time in world history, this centre in the heavens is marked by *Al Ruccaba*, the seventh (or first) star of Ursa Minor. In Vedic literature this Pole Star and its constellation is associated with the summit of Mount Meru, the seat of the gods, which is situated at the North Pole.[70] As the motionless guiding star of the north for mariners and travellers, it became known as the Lodestar, mentioned by Helena in Shakespeare's *Midsummer Night's Dream*: 'Your eyes are lodestars, and your tongue's sweet air more tuneable than lark to shepherd's ear.'[71]

An early Greek name for the constellation was *Phoenice*, 'the Beautiful', from which the Phoenicians derived their name. Like the Phoenicians, the phoenix owes its appellation to this title, the fabulous bird being essentially a dove with a purple-red breast and crest denoting its love and illumination. The Phoenicians were associated with Arcadia, and Arcadia was linked with Phoenicia (Ursa Minor). In Greek legend the great Arcadian hero was Arcas, the son of Zeus and the beautiful Callisto. When he died he was raised to heaven to become Ursa Minor, the Little Bear. His mother, Callisto, became Ursa Major, the Great Bear. The Arcadians were known as the Bear Race.

Not only was Arcas revered as the good Shepherd and associated with the whole sheepfold of Ursa Minor, but he was also identified with *Al Ruccaba,* the North Pole Star. As such he personifies the gate and gatekeeper of the sheepfold.

The Phoenician symbol of a phoenix or dove is emblematic of peace, just as the sheepfold is also the sign of peace. This is a common theme in many traditions and is still used today. Another ancient symbol of peace is the olive tree, the oil of which is traditionally used in the anointing unguent for bishops and kings, and the branch of which is carried by the dove of peace. The mention of olive trees surrounding the sheepcote confirms and embellishes the meaning that Shakespeare intends, as well as the description of the 'murmuring stream', a beautiful metaphor for the river of life which softly murmurs the Word of love.

Therefore, in this grand symbolism of Shakespeare's, the Duke's cave represents the Occult Pole, heart centre of the ecliptic and its Zodiac, whilst the shepherd's cottage and sheepcote signifies the North Pole Star, heart centre of the northern hemisphere at this period in time. The Occult Pole is the truly still point in the heavens, which the Celestial North Pole circumambulates, just as Shiva's Shakti (his feminine and active counterpart) is said to dance around her stationary lord in the Hindu tradition.

9. The Characters

Meanings & Mythology of Names

In all his plays, Shakespeare names his characters—or most of them—with great care, so that the names tell something about the character and the role which that character plays. This is not only a good dramatic aid, but it follows the ancient tradition that a person's name should tell something about that person and what that person's purpose is in life, or what he or she is to learn. It is a sacred and serious business to name a child correctly. Moreover, when undergoing initiation (*e.g.* baptism), which entails a psychological rebirth, a new 'spiritual' name (*e.g.* Christian name) is often given. This new name is usually given under inspiration or as the result of a vision or dream, or intuitively. Sometimes the spiritual name forms a contrast to the natural name given at the time of natural birth: sometimes it complements or enhances the natural name.

One example of this from the Christian tradition is that of Simon Peter. The disciple's original name was Simon (Hebrew *Shim'on* or *Simeon*), which means 'one who hears', whereas Jesus gave him the name Peter (Greek *Petros*, Hebrew *Cephas*) directly after Simon had seen and recognised Jesus as the Messiah. Peter means both 'the rock' and 'one who sees and knows', for 'the rock' refers to the strength (*Boaz*) of understanding and clear perception. This strength is represented by the left-hand pillar of Intelligence or Strength that constitutes the foundation upon which the Church or Temple of Wisdom is built. Moreover, the two names, natural and spiritual, of Simon Peter refer to the fact that one needs to first develop the intuitional hearing of the inner voice of wisdom before one can see and understand that voice clearly. 'The rock' is a traditional symbol and name of the hierophant of a temple or mystery school, and Simon Peter was made the hierophant of the twelve apostles and the other disciples in Jesus' school.

Besides these simpler facts, a whole mythology lies behind the names and roles, which helps to explain them even better. So, with this in mind, let us explore the meanings of the names in Shakespeare's *As You Like It*.

Rosalind

In Spanish, *Rosalind* means 'fair as a rose'. The Oxford Dictionary of English Christian Names derives it from the Old German *Roslindis*, 'horse-serpent'. However, *Rosalind* literally means 'Rose-Serpent', compounded from Latin *rosa*, 'rose', and *lind*, 'flying serpent' or 'dragon' (*e.g.* as in lindworm). *Lind* is an English word associated with *linn*, 'waterfall' or 'cascade', from the Celtic word *llyn* (Welsh) or *linne* (Gaelic); for the dragon was (and still is) a name for the fundamental etheric energy of nature, which flows like water. In Hindu teachings this same energy is called *shakti* or *kundalini*—Shakti being the bride or spouse of the god or lord who is usually addressed as Shiva. In Chinese *Feng Shui* this etheric energy is called *ch'i*. In Christian teachings it is called the fountain of life, for the fiery 'water' first rises up the spine (to marry with its 'lord' who is seated in the crown of the person) before it arches over and falls as a blessing, creating thereby an aura of celestial beauty.

Lind or *linn* is used as the name for the linden or lime tree—the dragon tree—which represents grace, beauty and happiness. The linden also signifies purity and is a protection against impure things. Its leaves are heart-shaped and its flowers are reputed to be a cure for epilepsy. Those who sit under lime trees are said therefore to be healed to some extent, or even cured, of such 'electrical storms'. The protective use of lime trees is derived symbolically from the sweet, sticky substance which the tree exudes, to which flies and such-like insects stick—flies being symbolic of Beelzebub and all his demonic creatures. In Shakespeare's *Tempest*, for instance, Prospero's cell is protected by lime trees. Prospero strings a line between these, on which he hangs rich or 'gaudy' clothes, and it is these clothes and the line they are hung on, and the lime trees, which stop the would-be murderers—who are first and foremost thieves—from carrying out their deadly mission. Parodying Freemasonic terminology, they say they wish to 'steal by line and level'. Shakespeare puns with the words *linn* and *line*, implying in this context the line or boundary dividing the pure from the impure. The horizontal line represents the material world, whilst the vertical line signifies the spiritual world. In Freemasonry the vertical line is held to be a measure of a person's uprightness of life and justness of intentions.

In the Rosicrucian wisdom tradition, when the serpent of our inherent nature is made to rise straight up the spine, like sap in a tree, it blossoms as a rose. This refers to the opening or blossoming of each of the chakras (*i.e.* the energy centres) on the spine, but, most importantly, the heart and crown chakras. The whole rose bush, in blossom, signifies this state of initiation and illumination, which is the state of beauty. In Christian tradition, the Virgin Mary is referred to as the Rose. The Mystic Rose, like the Rose of Dante, refers to the pure and beautiful soul—the one who can give birth to the Christ child or spiritual soul. In the Greek Mysteries, the pure and beautiful soul was called Persephone, the daughter of Zeus and Demeter. Persephone's child was named Dionysus, or Bacchus, who represented Illumination and Joy. Her mother, Demeter, was known as the great goddess of Nature and signified Harmony.

In *As You Like It,* Rosalind's character is entirely in keeping with this symbolism. She is what her name describes. When, in the Forest of Arden, she takes on the guise of Ganymede, she maintains the symbolism.

Ganymede was known to the Greeks as the most beautiful of all mortals. He was carried off by Zeus (in the form of an eagle) to become the great Olympian's cup-bearer. Translated into Celtic-Christian allegory, Ganymede became the Grail King. His feminine counterpart, Rosalind herself, is the Grail Queen—his own 'mother' and wife. The Grail Queen is the Holy Grail, the vessel of pure beauty and love, bearer of the shining knowledge of truth.

In Spenser's *Shepheard's Calendar,* Rosalind is Colin Clout's beloved, the mistress of his love. According to his own explanation, the poet masks himself under the character of Colin Clout, which means that Spenser's Rosalind is, like Dante's Beatrice,[72] a personification of the celestial rose, the poet's own heavenly soul and holy grail. Something of that is unquestionably present in Shakespeare's Rosalind.

Orlando

Orlando is the hero who wins Rosalind's heart and marries her. He is referred to as 'Signior Love' (III, ii, 286-287), and the spirit of his father is strong within him (I, i, 21-22, 70-71). *Orlando* is the Italian form of *Roland*, and Roland is the name of Orlando's father. The name means 'fame of the land'. It was the name of the legendary hero of the medieval *Chanson de Roland*, who was the nephew and the most famous of the peers of the Emperor Charlemagne. The name and story was made famous in the Renaissance by Ariosto's *Orlando Furioso*.

Celia finds Orlando under an oak tree, 'like a dropped acorn'; to which Rosalind replies, 'It may well be called Jove's tree, when it drops such fruit' (III, ii, 230-233). In Greek mythology, the oak was the symbol of Philemon, who was turned into an oak by Zeus when he died. His wife, Baucis, who died at the same time, was converted into a linden or lime tree (see 'Rosalind'). They had been particularly blessed and rewarded by Zeus because, when they were old and infirm, and lived in a small cottage, they gave the best of all they had to entertain Zeus and Mercury. Zeus was so pleased at their love and generosity that he metamorphosed their dwelling into a magnificent temple, and appointed Philemon and Baucis as its priest and priestess. After death, as trees, they stood as the twin pillars before the entrance of the temple.

Zeus, or *Iu-Pater* (Jupiter), is the 'Father of Light'. He represents divine love as mercy, compassion, generosity—qualities which Orlando displays. The oak is his tree emblem.

Celia

The Italian name *Celia* means 'heaven-born' or 'heavenly', from the Latin *caelestis*, 'heavenly', and *caelestia*, 'heavenly bodies'. The English name *Celia* is, however (according to the Oxford Dictionary of English Christian Names), probably as a rule a form of *Cecilia*, Latin *Caecilia*, the name of a celebrated Roman family. In English the name was usually written as *Cisely*, from which the family name of *Cecil* is derived.

In Spenser's *Faerie Queene,* Celia is the wise governor of the House of Holiness—'an ancient house renowned throughout the world for sacred love'. It is the house to which Una (Truth) brings the Red Cross Knight (Holiness) for healing and restoration.[73] Celia is the mother of Faith, Hope and Charity in Spenser's tale, and therefore has a correspondence in Greek mythology to the virgin goddess, Pallas Athena, the upholder of justice and virtue, the protectress of the brave, valorous and righteous, and the goddess of peace and learning.

Oliver

Oliver means 'man of peace and good-will', from the root word, *olive*. The olive tree is a symbol of this, and its oil is used as the anointing unction, symbolic of illumination. In French the name is *Olivier*, usually understood as derived from the French *olivier* or *oliver*, 'olive-tree', from the Latin *olivarius*. Another derivation is from the Old Norse *Olvaerr*, meaning 'kind, affectionate one'. It is clear, in the story, that these are the very qualities which Oliver lacks at first, or negates through his hatred of his youngest brother; but after his conversion, through the charitable action of Orlando, he quickly begins to fulfil the meaning of his name.

Like Roland (*i.e.* Orlando), Oliver was another of the famous peers of Charlemagne.

Jaques

There are two Jaques in the play: (a) a lord who attends on the exiled Duke, and (b) the second son of Sir Rowland de Boys. Both are deep thinkers: the former being a libertine turned melancholic who sold his lands in order to travel and learn from studying other people, and the latter being a scholar who gains his learning at university.

Jaques is the French form of *James* or *Jacob*. The name is derived from Hebrew *Ja'akob*, 'a heel', referring to Jacob who took his brother Esau by the heel in the womb. It also means 'supplanter', as Jacob supplanted Esau as the son who received the blessing from their father Isaac. But these meanings are disputed. Just as meaningful would be 'cunning', for this was the characteristic behaviour of the patriarch Jacob, who gained both the birthright and the blessing by use of his intelligence.

A better guide, perhaps, is gained from the disciples of Jesus, of whom there were two of that name: (a) James the son of Zebedee (*i.e.* James the Great), and (b) James the Just, son of Alphaeus (*i.e.* James the Less). The latter took the place of the former when James the Great was beheaded: so that there was always a trinity of apostles heading the early group of Jesus' disciples, composed of Peter, James and John. The symbol of James the Great became the sword by which he was martyred, and in Christian iconography he is traditionally placed on the left of any grouping, balancing Peter who is normally positioned on the right. Peter holds the hierophant's keys as the emblem of his office, whilst James holds the sword of his martyrdom, which is also the double-edged sword of truth. This symbolism portrays Peter as representative of the right-hand pillar of Wisdom and Mercy, and James as representative of the left-hand pillar of Intelligence and Justice (or Righteousness). This identification is in fact continued by James the Just, for he was renowned for his religious purity and highly disciplined holiness of life, and as being a truly righteous man.

The two Jaques would seem to be some kind of echo of the two Jameses, and they in turn seem to have something in common with the idea of the Gemini—the twins, Castor and Pollux, of whom Esau and Jacob are biblical equivalents. Pollux is the heavenly or immortal brother, whilst Castor is the earthly or mortal twin. The two demonstrate the two basic ways of learning—academic and experiential. The duality also relates to how the mind works in order to see and understand, using reason and imagination, or analysis and conceptualisation, which the double-edged sword symbolises. Moreover, Gemini is an Air sign, ruled by Mercury, the messenger of thought.

Duke Frederick

Frederick is derived from Old German *Frithuric*, 'peaceful ruler', compounded of *frithu*, 'peace', and *rich*, 'ruler'.

Adam

Adam is, of course, the name of the first of mankind, originally bisexual. The name *Adam* is of Hebrew origin and is related to the Hebrew word *adamah*, 'red earth', the fiery substance from which Adam was formed. The word *man* means 'the thinker', which is the mind or intelligence, hence Adam is the name given to that form of intelligence which we call human—in other words, the human soul.

In the Hebraic text of the scriptures, the hermaphrodite Adam becomes known as *Aish*, meaning 'a man of substance or worth', when Eve (Hebrew *Aishah*) is separated from the male *Aish*.[74] In translations, however, the name 'Adam' is reapplied to the male principle, *Aish,* and consequently both Adam and man have come to represent the male faculty as well as the hermaphrodite condition. Adam is associated with the Garden of Eden, which contains an orchard in which is the tree of knowledge (apple tree) and tree of life (date palm). His work was to serve the garden as its gardener.

In the play, Adam is first encountered in the orchard of Oliver's garden, as the faithful old servant of the deceased Sir Roland de Boys. Not only does Adam become Orlando's servant and companion in exile, but he also gives Orlando his life's savings, amply fulfilling the meanings of his name.

Dennis

Dennis is a servant of Oliver de Boys. His name is derived from Latin *Dionysius,* Greek *Dionysos,* which literally means 'Son of God'.

Touchstone

Touchstone is Duke Frederick's fool, who is greatly attached to Celia and runs away with her and Rosalind. *Touchstone* is the name given to a hard, dark siliceous stone, such as basalt or jasper, that is used to test the quality of gold and silver. This is done by observing the colour of the streak each metal produces when rubbed on the touchstone. Morally, or philosophically, it signifies a criterion or standard by which judgment can be made in respect of love (gold) and thought (silver). This is precisely the role of a good professional fool. In the human individual it corresponds to the conscience.

Audrey

Audrey is the goatherd who marries Touchstone. Her name *Audrey* means 'noble strength'—the strength to overcome life's difficulties. It is derived from Anglo-Saxon *Æthelthryth* or *Etheldreda*.

Corin

The name of Corin the shepherd seems to be a form of *Corwin*, 'heart-friend', derived from Old Franco-English *cor-wine*, 'heart-wine'.

Silvius

Silvius means 'wood-dweller'. It is derived from the Latin *Sylvanus*, the deity of fields and forest, and is a name of Pan, the spirit of Nature. Pan is known as the protector of flocks, herds, forests, streams, *etc.*. Silvius, in the play, is a shepherd, one of the principal roles of Pan.

Phebe

Phebe, or Phoebe, is the goddess of the moon. Derived from the Greek *Phoebe*, it means 'bright one'. It is the feminine counterpart to *Phoebus*, 'radiant', the title of the sun-god Apollo.

William

William is derived from the Old German *Willahelm*, 'resolute protector', compounded of *vilja*, 'will', and *helma*, 'helmet'.

10. Tree of Life

The Cabala and Shakespeare

The Shakespeare plays embody a deep knowledge of Hebraic-Christian Cabala, therefore it is sometimes helpful to see how the characters of a play as well as the locations relate to each other in terms of what is called the Cabalistic 'Tree of Life'.

As we have already seen, the locations and the names of the characters have been carefully chosen by Shakespeare, and each character embodies certain characteristics and qualities, be they virtues or vices, strengths or weaknesses. These qualities may be apparent or hidden, well developed or in embryo. All these characters are then put together by Shakespeare in particular situations, in which they relate to each other in various ways and produce a variety of responses and effects. All the characters and situations may well be drawn from life—as that is assuredly what Shakespeare did, since they are so real to us—but they are not haphazard or chaotic, for life is not haphazard or chaotic. This is surely, I believe, what Shakespeare is trying to show us—the fact that behind everything is a fundamental law of life that produces order out of chaos and yet allows us a relative freedom of choice and movement.

The study of psychology shows that such patterns do exist in the human psyche, just as structures certainly exist in the natural world. The Cabala goes further and reveals the spiritual archetypes or causes that lie behind the psyche, and even the divine world that lies behind the spirit. There is a science of god-names, for instance, which concerns the various aspects of Divinity and how they both manifest and operate in the 'worlds' of the spirit, the psyche and nature. The original Hebrew version of the Bible included the Hebraic god-names, but when it was translated into more modern languages these were gradually replaced by more general names, until in the final versions of the Bible that we have today, and which the Elizabethans had, we are left only with names like God or Lord to cover everything. Then the Elizabethan authorities went a step further and banned even the mention of 'God' in all plays. In one way this undoubtedly helped Shakespeare and other playwrights, since they made recourse to the Classical names of gods and goddesses, which belong to another version of the same basic Cabala—a version which has been passed on and developed via Neoplatonism.

In the Renaissance it was considered to be entirely appropriate and no threat to religion to use the Classical names and talk about the Classical gods and goddesses, heroes and heroines, and the various myths and legends surrounding them. Shakespeare has made full use of this and, with consummate skill, has created Mystery plays that use and embody Neoplatonic Cabalistic knowledge. However, it helps to know the 'language' of this science, and the so-called 'Tree of Life', presented in the form of a diagram, is a key to this. It is like an architect's drawing, but in this case it is the design of the universe created by the

Grand Architect of all, as periodically revealed to the great prophets and seers, and interpreted to mankind in the first instance by Enoch.[75]

In *As You Like It* this Tree of Life structure of characters and locations can be seen fairly clearly, but it is important to note that there is more than one way in which the relationships of characters can be meaningfully shown on the Tree of Life diagram. This does not mean that the arrangements are necessarily haphazard or that one can make any arrangement one likes. This is definitely not so. Every possible arrangement is meaningful and has to be meaningful, but there are usually different arrangements for different levels of the psyche. How one appears to others, for instance, may be very different to how one is within one's heart. How we each are expected to behave in society may be very different to the psychological reality. Some men, for instance, who are sexually men, may be psychologically feminine, whilst some women, who are sexually women, may have a strong masculine psychology. Likewise, some seemingly gentle people have turned out to have hearts of steel, whilst many warriors have proved to have kind hearts.

In this chapter I describe three different arrangements for the characters and two alternatives for the locations on the Tree of Life. They are almost certainly not the only arrangements that can be made, but I offer them as examples of how the play is structured in this way, as a dramatised reflection of human society. Before doing this, however, a brief description of the Cabalistic Tree of Life might help those who are unfamiliar with this key teaching in our Hermetic wisdom tradition.

Description of the Tree of Life

'The Tree of Life' is the name for a unique diagram, based on sacred geometry, which depicts the harmonious order and structure of the universe. It is both a symbol of truth and a key to discover truth. Although there are many ways to interpret it, the Tree represents and reveals the basic harmony and order that lies behind all things. It is like a formula—an equation showing how the various laws and expressions of life balance and harmonise in one whole. Through the Tree we can discover how different characters, for instance, relate to each other, and how different psyches and situations can be balanced, harmonised and resolved into a conscious and illumined whole. Life exists because of polarity, and the Tree shows the various inter-dimensional polarities of life.

The Tree of Life, as a teaching aid and formula for truth, is generally said to be Hebraic in origin. However, its principles can be found in other wisdom traditions, such as the Ancient Egyptian, the Classical and the Christian. It is through the Jewish and Christian Cabala that it is mainly known. As a result of Pico della Mirandola and Marsilio Ficino's partnership in the 15th century, Christian Cabala became an integral part of Renaissance Neoplatonism. It is upon this that Shakespeare drew and in which he was well versed.

The Four Worlds

The basic Tree of Life diagram shows the divine principles of life in their relationships to each other. Each principle is connected to others via pathways, making a network or pattern of life that exists in what are known as the Four Worlds of Existence. These Four Worlds are known in

Tree of Life

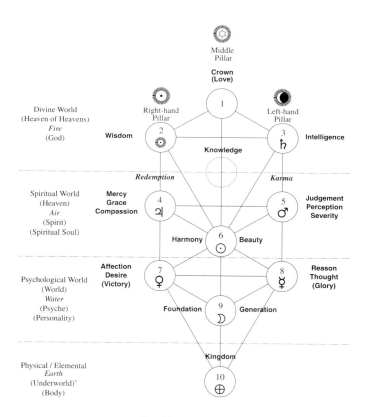

Middle Pillar

Crown
(Love)

Divine World
(Heaven of Heavens)
Fire
(God)

Right-hand
Pillar

Left-hand
Pillar

1

Wisdom

2

3

Intelligence

Knowledge

Redemption

Karma

Spiritual World
(Heaven)
Air
(Spirit)
(Spiritual Soul)

Mercy
Grace
Compassion

4

5

Judgement
Perception
Severity

Harmony

6

Beauty

Psychological World
(World)
Water
(Psyche)
(Personality)

Affection
Desire
(Victory)

7

8

Reason
Thought
(Glory)

Foundation

9

Generation

Kingdom

Physical / Elemental
Earth
(Underworld)*
(Body)

10

THE TREE OF LIFE

Cabala as the World of Emanation, the World of Creation, the World of Formation and the World of Action or Fact. In Neoplatonism they are usually referred to as the Divine, Spiritual, Celestial and Terrestrial Worlds. As a key to understanding and discovering correspondences, the alchemical symbols of Fire, Air, Water and Earth are given to these four worlds respectively. The Tree of Life exists

191

complete in all of them, for the four worlds are the four phases of the Divine, as represented by the Tree of Life, coming into existence and expressing Itself so that It might be known and enjoyed. The process of life—*i.e.* impulse-desire-thought-action—is based on this and is a guide to understanding what the Four Worlds are.

1. The Divine World. The Divine World or World of Emanation is a Unity—one Existence that is the source and impulse of all manifestation. This Unity contains ten divine principles (Hebrew, *sephiroth*). These are the principal potentialities of expression contained within the Divine Unity. Moreover, it is always emphasised in Cabala that there are ten principles, no more and no less. Together they form the fundamental 'mathematical' equation for the whole universe, from which all else is derived.

For instance, God is One yet Three-in-One, for all manifestation only occurs through polarity and the relationship between the two poles—hence three, yet one. Likewise, the Trinity-in-Unity (or Holy Trinity) manifests itself in three phases, the potential for which exists as principles in the Divine World. The three Trinities plus their essential Unity comprise the ten principles.

The essential Trinity is Divine Being that is both Father and Mother of all expression of life—which is and can only be the expression of Itself. This Divine Being is Love in its absolute sense, and it is this love which exists as the relationship between the polarities of what are called the Father and Mother. The Father aspect is God and the Mother aspect is Goddess, yet they are one single All-Good (from which the name *God* derives).

Various other names are used to describe the Holy Trinity, depending on which set of principles are being referred to. The first set of principles, describing the Absolute, are usually named Crown (*i.e.* Love), Wisdom and Intelligence. The second set can be summarised as Mercy, Judgment and Beauty; the third as Desire, Thought and Action (*i.e.* the power of Generation). These are all combined as one in the Kingdom, the tenth principle that describes the final, full manifestation of the Absolute Divinity, which is at the same time Divinity's field of action.

2. The Spiritual World. Each divine principle manifests as an Archetype or Archangel in the spiritual World of Creation. This world is the realm of the Word[76] and the Holy Breath[77] which carries it.[78] This super-celestial world corresponds to the *Nous* in Hermetic literature, which is the *Pymander* or 'Good Shepherd' who looks after us, his 'sheep'.

An 'angel' is a divine idea (which is what *ang-el* means), which are sometimes referred to as spirits or intelligencies. Each of them gives form to a divine principle. However, the forms of the Archangels are the essential and creative forms of pure sound and light (*i.e.* the *Logoi*), as distinct from the more visual thought-forms of ordinary angels. As pure vibrating thoughts or ideas, which are direct expressions of love as the creative energy of love-wisdom, the Archangels inhabit the 'airy' realm of the universal mind. However, this universal mind is not the same as the personal mind we normally equate with the word 'mind'. It is rather the higher or spiritual mind which is in fact associated with the heart—the central, shining Sun of all Creation—the centre that is everywhere in a circle that is nowhere. This spiritual world is sometimes described as 'the heaven of heavens' (or 'the three heavens of heavens').

3. The Celestial World. The Archangels or *Logoi* are reflected (*i.e.* imaged) as thought-forms in the celestial World of Formation, the realm of the Soul; where, besides being heard, they can be seen. These thought-forms, created by the Word of God, include both angels and human souls, relating to each other in a beautiful and harmonious order that is basically hierarchical. This world is described as the Seven Heavens, and the organisation of creatures in it as the Angelic Order or Hierarchy. This hierarchy has itself ten subsidiary orders or hierarchies, and the soul of man is known as the tenth. However, the human soul, manifesting the idea of the Kingdom, has the unique potential to rise through the angelic hierarchy and heavens, its destiny being to attain the crown position in the seventh heaven in full knowledge and expression of God. To do this, the soul must incarnate in the terrestrial world in order to complete the divine process of manifestation and to gain full knowledge of life.

The seven heavens contain and are expressions of the ten divine principles and spiritual archetypes. They are known as the heavenly Paradise or Eden. There are different ways of relating the seven heavens to the Tree of Life with its ten principles; but, generally speaking and with respect to each other, the lowest three heavens are objective, the next three are subjective, and the highest heaven (the 'seventh heaven') is essential and 'three-in-one'. What is known as the natural human soul (psyche) belongs to the lowest three heavens, beginning in the first heaven. The upper three heavens are the dwelling place of the spiritual soul, whilst the seventh heaven is the final haven of the soul who has become 'like unto God', a manifestor of the Word of love.

The Celestial World also contains the shadow aspects of the seven heavens, known as the 'lower Eden', and in these are the seven 'hells', the planes of purgatory. All these are but temporary residences until the souls therein can purify and release themselves from their self-imposed conditions.

4. The Terrestrial World. The terrestrial and sensory World of Action or Fact is the physical universe and, for us, our physical globe. To the Greeks it was the underworld. It is the realm of Nature, into which souls (of humans, animals, plants, *etc.*) incarnate from the celestial sphere and take on earthly bodies. The earth plane is the final and outermost manifestation of life, the 'echo' of the celestial and spiritual realms: which is one of the reasons why the ancient sages used to say that all nature is but a symbol of psychological truths and spiritual realities. On earth, ideas can be put into action in dense matter, and that matter can be transformed and transmuted into finer and eventually subtle form as a result. Just as there are seven heavens above, so there are seven earths or earthly planes of existence.

The Geometry of the Tree of Life

The geometry of the Tree of Life is the same geometry that governs the design of sacred buildings. Therefore, the Tree is often associated with the Temple of Light, or Temple of Solomon. For instance, if you look at the diagram of the Tree, you will notice immediately that it has three vertical axes. These are known as the pillars of the temple. You will also see that there are what are known as the ten *sephiroth* or principles, each represented by a small circle and a number, 'hanging' on those pillars. Sometimes these are called 'fruits' of the Tree of Life. If you look further, you might notice that these ten *sephiroth* are disposed in three sets of three, like triangles, with the final *sephira* on its own at the base.

There are different ways to understand all this. As described so far, the complete Tree of Life is present in every world of existence—divine, spiritual, celestial and natural, microcosmically as well as macrocosmically. Hence it is said in the Hermetic teachings, 'As above, so below': only what is below is in the process of responding to, embodying and mirroring as well as it can that which is shining upon it from above.

However, another way of understanding the Tree is to see all four worlds represented in one Tree of Life pattern. In such a representation, the lowest *sephira,* numbered '10' in the scheme, signifies the world of nature—the lowest and densest realm of existence. This corresponds to our physical bodies. The set of three *sephiroth* (nos. 7-9) immediately above this 10th *sephira* corresponds to the celestial world of our psyche. Above this are the three *sephiroth* (nos. 4-6) representing the super-celestial world of the spirit, and at the very top, crowning the Tree, are the three (nos. 1-3) that signify the Holy Trinity of the divine world. In ascending order, therefore, these four groups are symbolised by the alchemical elements of earth, water, air and fire.

The Tree of Life in the Shakespeare Plays

In the context of the Shakespeare plays, the psychological viewpoint is probably the most interesting and apparent, although behind the psyche lie the spiritual qualities and divine principles that the psyche is trying to manifest. Occasionally in the plays, Shakespeare makes direct reference to the spiritual realities by introducing (or mentioning) gods and goddesses, or angels, to represent them. As for the divine principles, they are laws of the universe: these are always present, unseen but governing the story of every play. At moments of great import, such as Portia's speech about mercy in the trial scene of *The Merchant of Venice,* Shakespeare makes known these principles with breath-taking power, revealing the true majesty, poetry and wisdom of divine love.

The Tree gives us a map of the psyche, and on this map the various characters of the play can be fitted into their appropriate places (although, being human, none is ever fixed or perfect, or just one simple type). This gives us a structure of society about which Shakespeare is telling us in the play. Furthermore, if we grasp the fact that the whole Tree is also in ourselves, then we will be able to see that each character in the play represents an aspect of our own psyche, and that the Tree is a structure of our own self. Orlando and Oliver are part of each of us, as are Rosalind and Celia, Touchstone, Jaques, and the two Dukes, *etc..* They live in us and we have to deal with what that means.

In Christian Cabala, the Tree is shown in a heraldic way, facing us as we look at it, whereas in Jewish Cabala it is shown the other way round, with us looking at it from behind: otherwise it is exactly the same Tree. In the diagrams included here, the viewpoint of the Christian Cabala is used. If you were to look straight-on at the stage of the Globe theatre, for instance, as a member of the audience, you would see (in a vertical context) the Tree of Life represented by the stage and its twin pillars from the Christian cabalistic viewpoint. Likewise, each actor on that stage, when facing you, would represent that same Tree of Life in microcosm.

Locations on the Tree

The Two Pillars

As already mentioned (Chapter 8, 'The City and the Forest'), the locations of city and forest can be seen to represent aspects of the Tree of Life in two main ways. The first way is with the city symbolising the left-hand 'lunar' pillar and the forest signifying the right-hand 'solar' pillar. The city is a good symbol of the left-hand pillar of Intelligence and Justice because it is associated with the human intelligence or soul (symbolised by the Moon), and is highly structured and ruled under stringent man-made laws and social codes of conduct. Contrasting this, the forest is outside the rigorous laws of the city and is relatively free as a result, being ruled primarily by the laws of nature which are a direct manifestation of the spiritual laws of the universe (symbolised by the Sun). In the forest wisdom reigns and can be discovered, unjust deeds can be redeemed, and situations can be transmuted to higher and more loving states of being: all of which makes the forest a suitable emblem of the right-hand pillar of Wisdom and Mercy.

Heaven and Earth

The second way is when the city represents the celestial world of the human soul and the forest connotes the physical world of nature into which human souls have to incarnate in order to resolve problems and develop love. When this has been done, the souls concerned can return home to their celestial 'mansion' with some knowledge and joy, making their Eden a little better than it was as a result. Because their Eden is not perfect, it is the Lower Eden, not the higher, which is being represented. In this arrangement the De Boys house and orchard are symbolic of the central orchard in the heart of Eden, whilst the palace belongs to a higher plane of Edenic existence.

The Celestial Eden

There is also a third arrangement worth considering, and this is when all the locations are treated as belonging to the celestial world of the psyche. In this case there is one Tree of Life—the celestial Tree, representing the Edenic Paradise, which itself has the four main levels symbolised by the alchemical elements. As the situations depicted are not by any means perfect, the Paradise is that of the Lower Eden, the 'shadow' or imperfect image of the Upper Eden.

In this arrangement, the forest suitably suggests the 'earth' level, equated with the principle of the Kingdom and the first (*i.e.* lowest) heaven. The first heaven is inhabited by human souls at the starting point of human evolution, represented in the play by the lower classes of society, the peasants and farmers, who live and work in the forest. Although belonging to the psychological realm, through symbolic analogy this first heaven has a correspondence with the terrestrial world, and in fact is called 'the veil' between heaven and earth in Cabalistic tradition. It is known theosophically as the etheric level, whose substance provides the etheric body (*i.e.* the *prana-maya-kosa* or 'prana-formed sheath' of Buddhism) which makes it possible for us to incarnate into and remain in the physical world. It forms the link between the physical and the celestial worlds.

The De Boys house and orchard belong to the next level up—the 'water' level of the celestial Tree in which are the second and third heavens of Eden. These heavens are inhabited by more evolved souls, who in the play are represented by the knights and gentlemen squires—the middle class. Through symbolic analogy, this level of the celestial world represents the whole celestial realm.

Above this is the palace, home of the courtiers and princesses, representing the 'air' level of Lower Eden, in which are the fourth, fifth and sixth heavens. In the Upper Eden this would be the home of the saints and masters. This 'air' level has a correspondence with the spiritual world.

At the highest level there is the unnamed location, the throne of the grand dukes, signifying the 'fire' level of the celestial Tree and seventh heaven of Lower Eden. In the Upper Eden this would be the throne of the Messiah or Christ. This 'fire' level has a correspondence with the divine realm.

Characters on the Tree (1)

One fairly obvious arrangement of the characters of *As You Like It* on the cabalistic Tree of Life is according to their social standing, in a social hierarchy, as in the third example given above of the locations used in the play.

Elizabethan society was strictly hierarchical, although it had become possible for individuals to rise up through the well-defined social hierarchy by means of their own efforts. It was a period when the middle classes were beginning to find their power. Many successful merchants climbed into the ranks of the gentry, and many gentlemen lawyers, knights and others became

Tree of Life

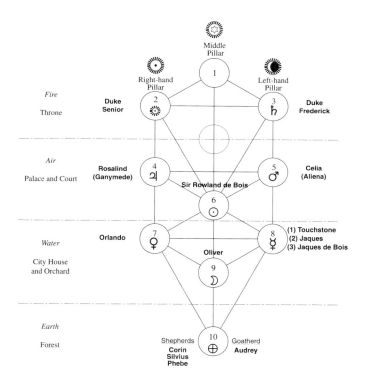

Middle Pillar

Right-hand Pillar

Left-hand Pillar

1

Fire

Throne

Duke Senior — 2

3 — Duke Frederick

Air

Palace and Court

Rosalind (Ganymede) — 4 ♃

5 ♂ — Celia (Aliena)

Sir Rowland de Bois

6 ☉

Water

City House and Orchard

Orlando — 7 ♀

8 ☿ — (1) Touchstone / (2) Jaques / (3) Jaques de Bois

Oliver

9 ☽

Earth

Forest

Shepherds / **Corin** / **Silvius** / **Phebe** — 10 ⊕ — Goatherd / **Audrey**

THE CHARACTERS ON THE TREE (1)

the new aristocrats and courtiers alongside the ancient nobility. The social hierarchy was part of the Elizabethan, and indeed Renaissance, world-view, inherited from the past and believed in by people generally, for with it came a measure of stability. Moreover, it was considered to be a reflection of the divine order in the heavens by means of which God administers the universe. This world-view is inherent in Shakespeare's plays and relates to the hierarchical structure of the Tree of Life.

For instance, the two Dukes naturally take the highest positions on the Tree, as polarities to each other. Duke Senior is representative of Wisdom, the light or solar principle which crowns the right-hand 'pillar' of the Tree, and Duke Frederick personifies the Intelligence, the reflective lunar principle which crowns the left-hand 'pillar' of the Tree. These brothers are antagonists to each other, like Antonio and Shylock in *The Merchant of Venice* who personify the principles of love and hate, until love can resolve the situation into one of harmony and friendship.

Directly beneath the two dukes on the Tree of Life come the princesses: Rosalind beneath her father, Duke Senior, and Celia beneath her father, Duke Frederick. In her position, Rosalind is representative of Mercy, symbolised by Jupiter, and of redemptive healing and wise teaching which are Mercy's attributes. As Ganymede, Rosalind emphasises her role on the Tree, for Ganymede is the beloved of Jupiter, who is taken up into heaven by Jupiter to become the cup-bearer of the gods. Rosalind's cousin Celia, by contrast, is her close friend and natural polarity at her 'level', having a clear perception and quick wit which are synonymous with the attributes of Judgment on the Tree of Life. Traditionally, Judgment is symbolised by Mars, signifying the divisiveness that is required in order to see clearly, setting one thing apart from another in order to analyse and make comparisons. Celia's pseudonym as Aliena ('the Alien' or 'Stranger') seems to be suitable for this role.

I would place the deceased Sir Rowland de Boys in the heart of the Tree of Life, the place of Harmony and Beauty, represented by the Sun. He is described as such by Rosalind when she says: 'My father loved Sir Rowland as his soul, and all the world was of my father's mind'

(I, ii, 224-225). This description is fitting for this central position, as the soul (*i.e.* heart or sun) of Wisdom.

Beneath him and the two princesses on the Tree come the three brothers of Sir Rowland, who make a trinity relating to intuitive love, intellectual learning and will power (see Chapter 4, 'Initiatory Themes'). These are appropriately matched to the three principles of Affection, Reason and Generation, symbolised respectively by Venus, Mercury and Moon. In addition, the melancholy Jaques fits the mercurial position of Reason, by name and character, as also does Touchstone, the court jester. These three—Touchstone, Jaques and Jaques de Boys—portray well the three levels of thought associated with mercurial reason: Jaques de Boys who learns from books in an academic way; the courtier Jaques who has learnt from books and goes on to study nature, through experience; and Touchstone who has learnt from both books and nature, and who has now the wisdom, wit and experience to be a professional fool or 'Mercury'.

The final position on the Tree of Life, the place of the Kingdom, is well personified by the shepherds and goatherds of the Arden Forest. There are three shepherds (Corin, Silvius and Phebe) and one goatherd (Audrey). They are related to each other symbolically as polar opposites: for instance, at the Last Judgment the sheep and the goats are separated from each other. According to Jesus' teaching,[79] the sheep go to the right-hand side of Christ and goats to the left. The sheep represent the saved, because they have demonstrated compassion, mercy and generosity. The goats signify the damned, who have not shown compassion, *etc.*, but on the contrary have acted selfishly and unlovingly.

Although this is an ancient teaching and one reiterated by Jesus, it is not the whole story, and puts the poor goat (and Audrey) in an unfavourable light, just as was done with the great god Pan who is represented so often as a goat and equated with the Devil. Sheep represent the right-hand side of the Tree of Life, associated with loving affection, mercy and wisdom, whilst goats are symbolic of the left-hand side of the Tree, associated with sharp wit, judgment and intelligence. Wisdom is Cupid, the Son of God, who is the Logos, Christ or Messiah, whilst Intelligence is Pan, the Son of Cupid.

The only thing is, it is the left-hand side of the Tree which is associated with the dark aspect of Creation. Its nature is material, severe, restrictive and separative, being the polarity to the spiritual expansiveness, freedom and all-embracing compassion of the right-hand side. However, without this restrictiveness, and the limitations which it brings, there would be no form, no individuality, nothing to identify, nothing to see or know. It is the darkness which enables the light to shine; the mind which can reflect and see the light; the matter which gives form to spirit; the righteousness which balances and makes holy (or complete) the passion of love; the discipline that regulates desire. It is the left side which is associated with the law of karma ('an eye for an eye, *etc.*'), whilst the right connotes the law of redemption ('be merciful…').[80] In an unevolved person or society, selfishness or tribal exclusiveness tends to dominate and the law of karma reigns supreme, with revenges and forms of apartheid perpetuating and exacerbating fears and hatreds. Ultimately, though, it is taught that when real love is practised, the law of redemption will transmute the law of karma, absorbing it into its grace so that both fear and revenge entirely disappear, as also will greed, selfishness, and social, racial and religious intolerance and discrimination. In its place there will be a purity of living, a responsiveness to love, and enlightened, visionary thinking.

MALE & FEMALE REPRESENTED AS SOLAR & LUNAR PILLARS

Characters on the Tree (2)

Another way that the characters of *As You Like It* relate to the Tree of Life is in terms of the pillars, as in the first example concerning the locations. Only, in this instance, it is the four couples who are married at the end of the play who make the arrangement. Two possible arrangements of this can be made, the first being with the men on the right and the women on the left.

Men to the right and women to the left is a very ancient and popular symbolism, where men are associated

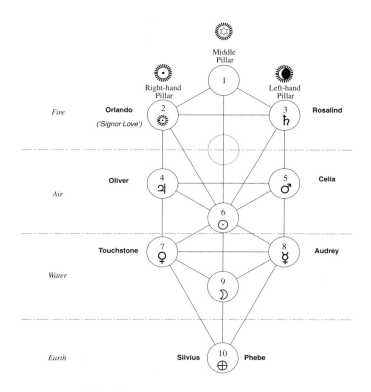

THE CHARACTERS ON THE TREE (2)

with the Sun and the solar pillar, and women with the Moon and the lunar pillar. The archetype of a male is traditionally perceived to be one of driving force, and that of a female as one of receptivity and responsiveness to that force, as manifested in the sexual differences. The male seeds the female and the female, receiving that seed, gives it form as a child. Corresponding to this, the right-hand solar pillar is traditionally known as the Pillar of

Force and the left-hand lunar pillar as the Pillar of Form. The forceful male principle is often represented by a straight line, standing stone or upright pillar, whilst the receptive female principle is portrayed by a circle which the line penetrates, a bowl in which the stone stands, or the very ground itself. In each individual, of whichever sex, both aspects are of course present, as each person embodies the whole Tree of Life. However, the sexual differences, from a cosmological point of view, are due to the basic archetypes of the right and left sides of the Divine Being, the Father (*Abba*) and the Mother (*Aima*).

Shakespeare clearly uses this arrangement in his play, as it is such a fundamental pattern in human relationships. Both the code of conduct of various societies around the world and the teachings of many religions are based on this, often with the unfortunate result of men being considered superior to women and the woman being required to obey the man in all things. Shakespeare goes out of his way in his plays to demonstrate what happens if men do not play the game properly, which would require them to embody the principles of wisdom, compassion and friendliness to all. In many cases he builds up the image of women so that they should seem, without breaking the traditional civil and religious code of relationships that was then in force, to be at least equal to men in quality and ability. Often, as with Rosalind and Celia in *As You Like It,* he portrays his heroines as starting off at a much higher level of evolution than the men, to which the men have to attain in order to 'win' their women.

The overall symbolism of this male-female relationship is hinted at by Shakespeare when Orlando is related to the fruit of the oak by Rosalind (III, ii, 230-233) and by Rosalind's name which associates her with the linden or lime tree (see 'Rosalind', Chapter 9). As in the story of Philemon and Baucis (see 'Orlando', Chapter 9), these two trees are symbolic of the two side pillars of the Tree of Life, which themselves are signified by the twin pillars at the entrance to Solomon's Temple. The 'dry' oak symbolises the right-hand solar or 'fire' pillar and the 'sticky' linden denotes the left-hand lunar or 'water' pillar.

Besides the sexual differences, the four couples have a hierarchical relationship with each other. Of all the lovers, Rosalind is the most important in social standing, as she is the daughter of the eldest and rightful Duke. After her comes Celia, as her cousin and the daughter of Duke Frederick. Their men are below them in social status and so, even though Oliver is older than Orlando, when Orlando marries Rosalind he is raised above his brother in the social hierarchy. He is also above his brother in soul evolution, and from that point of view he is an older soul than Oliver. These two couples are the highest in the marriage hierarchy, and so Orlando can be placed as Wisdom on the right-hand pillar and Rosalind as Intelligence on the left-hand pillar, whilst Oliver is located at Mercy (beneath Orlando) and Celia at Judgment (beneath Rosalind). In this arrangement, Orlando fulfils his title as 'Hercules' and 'Signior Love' by personifying Cupid, whilst Rosalind fulfils her name as the beautiful Psyche, Cupid's bride. Oliver earns his right to take up his position when he demonstrates love and generosity, and Celia is as she was in the previous 'Tree' example, virtuous and with a heavenly clarity and exactness concerning what is right or wrong.

Touchstone and Audrey are the next in social standing, for Touchstone is a court jester and therefore a courtier, although not one of the gentry. By marrying Touchstone, Audrey is raised in social standing from her original state as a member of the lowest class, a waged 'labourer' and a goatherd to boot, a position which was considered to be of the very lowest because of the goat's association with the devil. Touchstone's position as the bridegroom is as Affection on the right-hand pillar, and Audrey's position, as the bride, is as Reason on the left. Shakespeare carefully brings out the affection in Touchstone when he talks of his bride-to-be, as well as the more basic lust which is a lower attribute or shadow aspect of this Venusian principle. Audrey, on the other hand, is described as virtuous even though it sounds as if she is physically unattractive—although she is obviously attractive to Touchstone and her foulness might simply refer to her type of work. Virtuousness and chastity is a quality specifically associated with the left-hand pillar: but as for Mercurial wit, this Audrey has yet to learn.

Silvius and Phebe are the final couple, and as shepherd and shepherdess they belong to the lowest class and therefore the lowest principle on the Tree, the Kingdom. Phebe's name signifies the brightness of the moon, whilst Silvius' name recalls Pan, the spirit of nature. Together they are like the spirit and soul of the forest dwellers.

Characters on the Tree (3)

The second arrangement that can be made with the four couples is with them reversed—the women on the right and men on the left. Whilst the first arrangement, men on the right and women on the left, is the most basic and sexual level of relationship, which society as a whole recognises and models itself on, its reverse is a truth at a deeper level.

At this second, deeper level of the psyche it is the women who embody, or represent, the emotional and

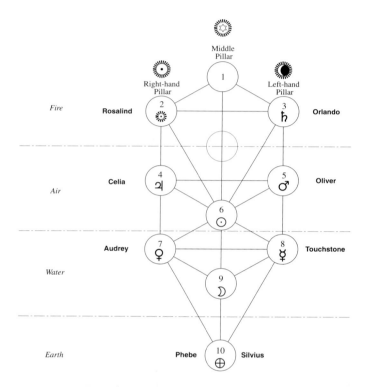

THE CHARACTERS ON THE TREE (3)

creative qualities of love—the wisdom, the compassion and the friendly affection. It is fairly natural for women to do so, especially in their role as mothers, and Shakespeare represents his heroines as doing just this. On the other hand, it is quite natural for men to be the protectors of their women and children, as warriors who hunt to provide for and who defend their families. Although society and religion chooses to use the other version of the Tree arrangement to organise itself by, yet at the same time it usually recognises this truth also, but without taking on board what it really means.

Shakespeare makes it very clear. Rosalind is the embodiment of loving wisdom: she loves wisely, speaks and teaches wisdom, and practices the magical use of love as a budding magus or magician. Celia is a perfect example of mercy, of loving self-sacrifice for her dearest friend, going bravely where she did not have to go and risking all kinds of dangers, including her father's wrath and schism from him and the home she probably loved. She recognises what is true and what is false, what is good and what is unjust, and out of love she supports the good and true. Audrey's position is also easy to see, for she provides a good example of what might be called 'Venusian' qualities in a simple, rustic way. She loves simply and honestly, yet clearly has a sensuousness and sexuality to which Touchstone is attracted.

From the men's point of view, Orlando acts like the intelligence which is hunting after truth, seeking its wisdom, its light, its love, and undergoing several tough adventures to attain its goal. Oliver likewise is a good match for Celia in the martial role of judgment, for he begins the play by acting severely and harshly towards his brother, judging things badly; but, after his conversion, he completely changes this to a clear perception of what is right to do. As for Touchstone, he is naturally the mercurial 'fool', the quick, sharp wit and messenger between all levels of society.

Silvius and Phebe take their positions at the foot of the tree, as shepherd and shepherdess, she to the right and he to the left.

Except for Silvius, the men are all courtiers who have become hunters in the forest, whilst the women, with the exception of Audrey, are or have become shepherdesses

THE
COVNTESSE,
OF PEMBROKES
ARCADIA.

WRITTEN BY SIR
Philip Sidney Knight.

NOW SINCE THE FIRST EDI-
tion augmented and ended.

LONDON.
Printed for William Ponsonbie.
Anno Domini. 1 5 9 3.

TITLE PAGE OF SIR PHILIP SYDNEY'S *ARCADIA*

in the more open pasture land. The shepherd or shepherdess is traditionally a symbol of the right-hand side of the Tree, signifying mercy, *etc.*, whilst hunters or warriors (and huntresses for that matter) are symbolic of the left-hand side, associated with the martial protective qualities of judgment, *etc.*. These are the two major symbols of Arcadia, as portrayed in the title page illustration of Sir Philip Sidney's *Arcadia*, which shows Musidorus on the right-hand side of the picture, disguised as a shepherd, and Pyrocles on the left, disguised as an Amazon. They are both men, with Pyrocles pretending to be a female Amazonian warrior, so the male-female relationship is different to Shakespeare's portrayal in *As You Like It*. However, the beautiful imagery on the title page of *The Whole Book of Psalmes* (1583), depicting a mother and child to the right and a male warrior to the left of the central title box, shows the Shakespearean point of view. Interestingly, this title page also has the Cupid headpiece at top and bottom of the page, which is an earlier and slightly simpler version of the 1623 Shakespeare Folio headpiece.

Conclusion

What I have presented is, I know, only a part of the picture, and there are certainly many more ways of seeing and interpreting such profound and wonderful works of philosophy and art as the Shakespeare plays are. Moreover, as the Cabalists would say, books of wisdom have four main levels and methods of interpretation: *Pshat*, 'simple', *Remez*, 'allusive', *Derash*, 'homiletic', and *Sod*, 'mystery', from the first letters of which is derived the name of Paradise (*PRDS*). All of them are enjoyable and instructive. I have not tried to deal with the simple level, except to give a brief background to the play. Whole libraries have

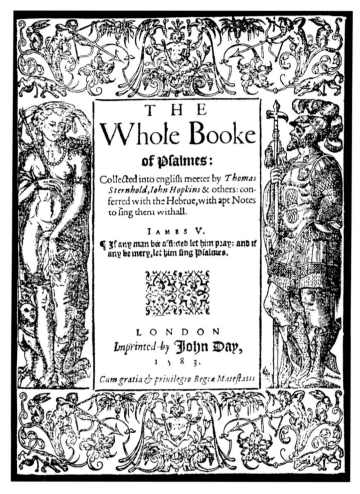

TITLE PAGE OF *THE WHOLE BOOK OF PSALMES* (1583)

been written on this score. What I have tried to do is to point a way into a study of the second and third levels, the allusive and homiletic. The fourth level, the mystery, cannot be written about: it can only be realised through experience and divine grace.

The Tree of Life is a marvellous aid to understanding relationships and the structure of society. It helps in understanding life, and it helps in understanding the structure of the play which is about life. It also gives us a glimpse into the structure of the universe, as perceived and agreed upon by the sages for thousands of years, and as given to mankind by direct revelation. To marry earth with heaven, by reflecting heaven on earth, has always been the goal of the great souls of humanity, as also is the purification of the celestial realms so that they may perfectly manifest and reveal the Word or Wisdom of God. The ultimate purpose of the human soul is to know God and rejoice in that knowledge: for, as ancient wisdom says, God is both lover and beloved, joy and the enjoyment of that joy.

Shakespeare gives us joy in his plays and poems. He also gives us a great deal to think about. Like his plays, there is more to him than meets the eye: and what a pleasure that is! My hope is that this book will help in some way to enhance that pleasure.

Notes on the Text

[1] Richard de Bury, High Chancellor of England, *A Vindication of [Epic and Dramatic] Poetry* (15th C.).

[2] The theory was proposed by J. H. Walter. See 'Introduction', *As You Like It,* The Arden Shakespeare, ed. Agnes Latham, p. xxvi.

[3] The existence of the letter was recorded by William Cory, Assistant Master at Eton, in his diary after a conversation with Lady Herbert. Cory was resident at Wilton at the time (August 1865), coaching Lady Herbert's son in Greek.

[4] P. Cunningham, *The Revels Accounts* (1842). See 'Introduction', *As You Like It,* The Arden Shakespeare, ed. Agnes Latham, pp. ix-x.

[5] See 'Introduction', *As You Like It,* The Arden Shakespeare, ed. Agnes Latham, p. xxxv.

[6] Mount Parnassus is actually dual-peaked.

[7] From *silex* was derived the term *Silentes*, the 'Silent Ones', a term used by the Pythagoreans to describe their initiates. The name of Silenus, the tutor and attendant of Bacchus, also comes from this source.

[8] Ed. Spenser, *The Faerie Queene,* Bk. 1, Prologue.

[9] Shakespeare, Sonnet 38.

[10] Ben Jonson, Tributary Poem, Shakespeare 1st Folio (1623).

[11] John Weever, *Epigrams in the Oldest Cut and Newest fashion* (*c.*1599).

[12] Thomas Lodge, 'To the Gentlemen Readers', *Rosalynde*(1592).

[13] 'Introduction,' *As You Like It*, The Arden Shakespeare, ed. Agnes Latham, pp. lix-lxv.

[14] The song first appears in Thomas Morley's *First Book of Ayres* (1600). Morley lived in Bishopsgate between 1596 and 1601.

[15] Since the Folio does not give a setting, the conventionally accepted settings are used. See The Arden Shakespeare. Theobald, *The Works of Shakespeare*, Vol. II (1733). N. Rowe, *The Works of Mr. William Shakespeare*, Vol. II (1709). Edward Capell, *Mr. William Shakespeare, his Comedies, Histories, and Tragedies*, Vol. III (1768).

[16] The time sequence appears to be erratic in the play. Here and elsewhere the story implies that the old Duke was banished many years previously—which must be at least twelve to fifteen years before, ever since the time when Celia was three years old, since that is the time from when Rosalind was always kept and brought up with her cousin. Yet, in Act 1, scene 1, the report by Charles, and, in Act 1, scene 2, Rosalind's depression at her father's banishment, seem to imply that the old Duke had only recently been banished.

[17] Shakespeare, *The Tempest*, IV, ii, 148-158.

[18] Shakespeare, *The Phoenix and Turtle*, v. 7.

[19] Francis Bacon, 'Of Goodness and Goodness of Nature,' *Essayes or Counsels, Civill and Morall* (1625).

[20] In this context, death does not necessarily mean physical death: it can refer to those who are dead spiritually. That is to say, they are dead in their love. Either they have subdued and killed their love, or it lies buried and unawakened. To be alive, on the other hand, means to be spiritually alive, which is loving. An initiate has to face death and remain alive, whilst transforming that which is dead into a state of life.

Notes on the Text

²¹ Plotinus, in a letter to his student Flaccus.

²² See the author's book in this series, *Shakespeare's Wisdom in The Merchant of Venice*. IC Media (1998).

²³ The position of the wounds and their relation to the life cycle arises as a result of how the zodiacal signs are related to the cycle of life. On the cycle of life, the culmination of the phase of desire or loving is marked by Taurus, which rules the throat; the culmination of the phase of thought or understanding is marked by Leo, which rules the heart; and the culmination of the phase of action or service is marked by Scorpio, which rules the sexual organs. (See the author's book, *Zoence, Science of Life.* Maine: Samuel Weiser – 1998.)

²⁴ For more details, see the author's book in this series: *Shakespeare's Wisdom in The Merchant of Venice*, ch 5. ICMedia (1998).

²⁵ Love–Word–Light, the three degrees of divine becoming, culminating in revelation (*i.e.* the seeing and recognising), are encapsulated in the 2nd and 3rd verses of the first chapter of *Genesis*:

> 1. And the spirit of God moved upon the face of the waters.
>
> 2. And God said, "Let there be light:"
>
> 3. And there was light.
>
> 4. And God saw that it was good: and God divided the light from the darkness.

²⁶ 'To be, or not to be, that is the question.' (*Hamlet*, III, i, 56).

²⁷ In this regard it is interesting that, in the biblical story of Jesus, Jesus said to Simon Peter, 'Get thee behind me, Satan,' immediately after Peter had challenged Jesus' forecast and decision to be

sacrificed (Matt. xvi, 23; Mark viii, 33). Moreover, Peter's challenge came immediately after he had been promised the keys of heaven by Jesus. St.Peter is represented as holding the keys of heaven and is known as the Doorkeeper in Christian tradition.

[28] See, for instance, *The Divine Pymander of Hermes Trismegistus*, p. 9, edited and published by The Shrine of Wisdom, 4th ed. 1955.

[29] Genesis i, 28.

[30] See G. R. S. Mead, *Thrice Greatest Hermes: Studies in Hellenistic Theosophy and Gnosis*, Vol. 1. Detroit, Hermes Press (1978). First printed by the Theosophical Publishing Society, London & Benares.

[31] Genesis i, 2.

[32] Genesis ix-x.

[33] To the observant, this should indicate that Shakespeare has also paired the eight sections or minor cycles of *As You Like It*: *i.e.* Earth-Moon, Mercury-Venus, Mars-Jupiter, and Saturn-Sun.

[34] Coffin of Petamon, Cairo Museum no. 1160. See Lucie Lamy, *Egyptian Mysteries*, p. 9, Thames & Hudson, 1981.

[35] Genesis i, 4.

[36] Ecclesiastes iii, 11.

[37] Ecclesiastes iii, 12-13.

[38] J. E. Harrison, 'Orphic Cosmogony', *Prolegomena to the Study of Greek Religion*, XII, 657. Cambridge University Press (1903).

[39] There are fourteen (*i.e.* seven plus seven) instances of this headpiece in the 1623 Shakespeare Folio, the other twelve

being headers to: *The Merry Wives of Windsor; Much Ado About Nothing; A Midsommer Nights Dreame; Twelfe Night, Or what you will; The life and death of King Iohn; The First Part of Henry the Fourth; The Second Part of Henry the Fourth; The Tragedy of Richard the Third; The Famous History of the Life of King Henry the Eight; The Tragedie of Romeo and Juliet; The Actors Names (in Tymon of Athens); The Tragedie of Hamlet, Prince of Denmarke.*

[40] For instance, the meaning of Israel (Is-Ra-El) is 'child of the Sun [Ra] of God [El]'.

[41] Luke ii, 34-35.

[42] Shakespeare, *A Midsummer Night's Dream*, I, i, 234-235.

[43] Shakespeare, *A Midsummer Night's Dream*, I, i, 239.

[44] Genesis i, 4.

[45] Francis Bacon, 'Cupid or the Atom, *The Wisdom of the Ancients,* translated from the Latin *De Sapientia Veterum* (1609). Spedding & Ellis, *The Works of Francis Bacon*, Vol. VI (1858).

[46] *i.e.* 'the Universe, or the All of things.' Francis Bacon, 'The First Example of Philosophy according to the Fables of the Ancients, in Natural Philosophy – Of the Universe, according to the Fable of Pan.' *De Augmentis*, Bk. 2 (1623).

[47] Francis Bacon, 'Pan, or Nature', *The Wisdom of the Ancients,* translated from the Latin *De Sapientia Veterum* (1623) – Spedding and Ellis, *The Works of Francis Bacon*, Vol. VI (1858).

[48] *Ibid.*

[49] This is not the original Cronos of the Orphic philosophers, who represented the Timeless Eternity of Dark Infinite Space that is the Origin of everything, including Eros-Phanes, the First-Born of Eternity.

[50] Francis Bacon, 'Cupid or the Atom,' *The Wisdom of the Ancients*, translated from the Latin *De Sapientia Veterum* (1609). Spedding & Ellis, *The Works of Francis Bacon*, Vol. VI (1858).

[51] 'In the beginning was the Word, and the Word was with God, and the Word was God. The same was in the beginning with God. All things were made by Him; and without Him was not anything made that was made. In Him was life; and the life was the light of men. And the light shineth in darkness; and the darkness comprehended it not.' – John i, 1-5.

[52] *Zohar* – Temurah 155a.

[53] '*Hoc enim [ie Philosophia] nos cum cæteras res omnes tum quod est difficilimum docuit; ut [nosmet ipsos] nosceremus, Cujus præcepti tanta vis, tanta sententia est, ut ea non Homini cuipiam, sed Delphico Deo tribueretur*' (*Cicero de Legib.*, lib. i.).

Thales, the Milesian, is said to have been the first author of the precept—γνῶθι σεαυτον —'Know thyself'. He is supposed to have said, that, 'for a man to know himself, is the hardest thing in the world' (see Stanley's *Life of Thales*). It was one of those precepts which Pliny affirms to have been consecrated at Delphos in golden letters. It was so frequently quoted that at length it acquired the authority of a divine oracle, and was supposed to have been given originally by Apollo himself. The opinion of its coming originally from Apollo was probably the reason that it was written in golden capitals over the door of his temple at Delphos. (See W. F. C. Wigston, 'The Chronicle Plays,' *Baconiana*, No. 28 [New Series], October 1899, p. 148.)

[54] A good parallel to place roles in terms of people roles is that of king, lord chancellor and lord chamberlain. The king personifies the divine ruler in the heart. The lord chancellor, who is the king's conscience or voice and the principal judge of the

kingdom, signifies the thinker in the head. The lord chamberlain, who is in charge of household matters, represents the governance of all abdomen functions.

55 'In my house are many mansions: if it were not so, I would have told you. I go to prepare a place for you.' John xiv, 2.

56 Genesis ii, 9.

57 Genesis iii, 16.

58 Genesis iii, 23.

59 Genesis ii, 15.

60 Genesis i, 26-29.

61 Encyclopaedia Britannica.

62 See France A. Yates, *Astraea*. Routledge & Kegan Paul (1975).

63 See the author's book, *Arcadia*, Pt. II, ch. 3, 'The English Areopagus and Arcadia'. FBRT (1988).

64 *Zodiac* means 'Circle of Creatures'.

65 The Arden Shakespeare, *As You Like It*, footnote to line 51, pp. 44-45 (1975 edition).

66 The Emerald Tablet (*Tabula Smaragdina*) of Hermes Trismegistos. For a good translation of the whole text, see Titus Burckhardt, *Alchemy*, ch.16, transl. from German by William Stoddart. London: Stuart & Watkins (1967).

67 John x, 1-5, 11, 14-16.

68 John x, 9.

69 E. W. Bullinger, *The Witness of the Stars*. Michigan: Kregal Publications (1980). Reproduced from 1893 Edition published in London.

R. Hinckley Allen, *Star Names – Their Lore and Meaning.* New York: Dover Publications (1963).

[70] Surya Siddhanta, I, v. 62, XII, v. 34.

[71] Shakespeare, *A Midsummer Night's Dream,* I, i, 183-184.

[72] See Dante (1265-1321), *Divina Commedia.*

[73] Ed. Spenser, 'The Legende of the Knight of the Red Crosse, or Of Holinesse,' *The Faerie Queene,* Bk 1 (1590).

[74] Shabaz Britten Best, *Genesis Revised.* Farnham: Sufi Publishing Co. (1964).

[75] It is said in Cabalistic tradition that Adam was first taught these truths by the great Archangel Raziel three days after he had been expelled from the Garden of Eden. Raziel, whose name means 'Secret of God', signifies the creative Wisdom of God. Enoch, however, was the first of mankind to realise these truths and therefore understand them fully. Hebrew tradition says that these truths, 'recorded' as Cabala ('the Received Truth' or 'Receiving'), were passed on via Noah, then in a line of descent via Abraham, Jacob, Levi, Moses and the Elders of Israel. Likewise, other traditions throughout the world have their line of descent of the same truths passed on from Enoch and Noah, expounded and reinterpreted in each age by the great teachers of mankind.

[76] Greek, *Logos,* Hebrew *Dabah.*

[77] Greek *Pneuma,* Hebrew *Ruach.*

[78] The Word and Breath constitute the Wisdom (Hebrew *Raisheeth*) which is translated as 'Beginning'. Hence, the opening verse of Genesis ('In the beginning God made the heavens and the earth') actually means 'In Wisdom God created the heavens and the earth'. Likewise, the opening verse

of John's gospel ('In the beginning was the Word…') means 'In Wisdom was the Word'.

[79] Matthew xxv, 31-46.

[80] See the author's book in this series, *Shakespeare's Wisdom in The Merchant of Venice*. I.C Media (1998).

Index

229